BEING

A Hiking Guide through Life

(from Frenzy to Serenity)

Philippe Erhard, M.D.

Copyright © 2010 by Dr. Philippe Erhard
First Edition – October 2010

www.erhard.ca
phil.erhard@gmail.ca

ISBN
978-1-77067-015-0 (Hardcover)
978-1-77067-016-7 (Paperback)
978-1-77067-017-4 (eBook)

∞

∞

Published by:

FriesenPress

Suite 300 – 852 Fort Street
Victoria, BC, Canada V8W 1H8
www.friesenpress.com

For information on bulk orders contact:
info@friesenpress.com or fax 1-888-376-7026

Distributed to the trade by The Ingram Book Company

Dedications

To Heather, my wife and best friend. Over the years, you have been my support and my coach. With you by my side - and because of you, I am a better person.

To physicians who have the privilege of helping the sick, a very rewarding but also demanding task.

I hope that this book will help them to stop, smell the roses and be a better healer to others and themselves.

Live life with a due sense of responsibility, not as those who do not know the meaning of life but as those who do.
Ephesians 5:15

The unexamined life is not worth living.
Plato

They could take everything from me except one thing and that was the attitude with which I chose to respond to the situation.
Viktor E. Frankl

What we play is life.
 Louis Armstrong

Everything has been figured out except how to live.
Jean-Paul Sartre

Oh to reach the point of death and realize one has not lived at all.
Henry David Thoreau

The only thing necessary for the triumph of evil, is for good men to do nothing.
Edmund Burke

Action may not always bring happiness, but there is no happiness without action.
Benjamin Disraeli

I have simply tried to do what seemed best each day as each day came.
Abraham Lincoln

Table of Contents

Introduction

This book was not supposed to be. After changing my work, I had more time in my life and thought it would be good to reread books I had found significant in the past. I was hoping that my reading would help me identify clear and practical goals or recipes on how to better manage my own life.

One night, I woke up with the outline of a book clearly in my mind. As sleep kept evading me, I had to get up and begin writing. Slowly, this book came to life. As it materialized, I realized that perhaps this knowledge would be helpful to others.

You may be familiar with most of the ideas presented here. What I have tried to do is present the information in a very practical and simple way. Something that can be applied to our daily, busy lives.

Drawing information from psychological studies, spiritual teachings, personal and professional experiences, I have tried to present a clear and easy, step-by-step pathway that will lead to a more balanced and peaceful life.

It will be especially useful for all of us who are overwhelmed by the busyness and speed of life, struggling to make some sense of our daily lives.

What can you learn from reading this book?

This book will help you to slow down, increase awareness of the present moment and develop a positive attitude in life.

You will learn that your body and your feelings are the key to your thoughts. You will also learn to make sense of your thoughts and control them in a positive way.

Reading this book is not enough. To have a real impact in your life, you need to follow the exercises presented at the end of each chapter. Most of these exercises are easy and simple to do, but need to be practiced daily for several weeks. It is the only way to change and renew your mind and life on a permanent basis...one small step at a time.

The ideas presented are arranged as follows:

- **The Basics (Physical Fitness and Breathing)**

- **Attitude, Gratitude and Mindfulness**

- **Awareness and Management of Feelings**

- **Mind Training (Meditation, Positive Thinking, and Flexibility)**

- **Reaching beyond Ourselves**

The story describes a hiking trip, where most of the events actually happened. Michael and Paul are imaginary people.

The hike takes place in the Vosges Mountains, in Alsace. This area is located in the east of France, just west of the German border. It is a magical area, full of history, beauty and culture. This is where I spent my youth and learned to appreciate the outdoors.

I hope this book will help you discover and develop the peace of slowing down, the joy of self-discovery, awareness of the present and enjoyment of the outdoors.

Have a good hike!

Acknowledgments

I would like to thank my wife, **Heather,** who was the first one to see the rough copy of this book and believe in it. She has been present throughout the process with guidance and support.

My thanks to **Ron Blicq** for professional help and guidance in developing this book. You not only gave me excellent advice, but have been an inspiration to me.

Thank you to **Marlene Van Helden** who did a superb job in reviewing and helping to edit this book.

Thank you to **Edna** and **Kaval Chohan**, and **Ruth Grewe** for their support and excellent advice.

Thank you to **John Klokow** for introducing me to meditation. Many thanks to **Lynn Lambert** for her help over the years.

Thank you to **Doreen Pendgracs and Karen McElrea** for their quality editing.

Thank you for **Marie Witt** and all the team at **FriesenPress** that made this book a reality.

Thank you **Matthew** and **Stephanie**, I have learned much from both of you. Matthew, for showing me how to enjoy life. Stephanie, for showing me what it means to live according to your beliefs.

And, of course, thank you to my **Mother** and **Father**. They are my inspiration for all of this.

I would also like to thank all the people who have crossed my path during my life. You may have written a sentence, a chapter or even more in the book of my life and helped me to become who I am today.

LEAVING

We must be the change we wish to see in the world.
Mahatma Gandhi

1

This is the shortest night of the year as the plane flies east toward the sun.

I'm finally relaxed, with nothing to do. I can just appreciate the present.

For the first time, I have a few hours of peace.

I've done it, finally!

I have quit!

After much agonizing indecision, I have finally decided to quit the rat race (or at least I hope to have quit).

In celebration, I am going to meet my old and good friend, Paul, and go on a hike.

The decision to change my life took a long time, but two things helped me decide.

I saw people around me wasting their lives hoping for an imagined future upon retirement.

I reread Viktor E. Frankl's book, *Man's Search for Meaning*.

After reading it, I knew I could not continue watching time pass me by without making a decision. I couldn't continue to rationalize my old way of living. I had to be responsible for my life and my decisions.

I did not enjoy questioning myself about the meaning of my life or how to live it. But Viktor Frankl is quite clear:

Be true to yourself.

I just had to answer two questions:

Do I have the courage to take a step in the direction I have always wanted to go?

Or do I accept my current situation, (which is quite acceptable in many aspects), and give myself up to the mirage of conformity and facility?

My mind is racing all over the place, like a wild horse. Now that my mind is free, it's hyperactive.

Maybe I should watch this in-flight movie; it may keep me focused.

No deadlines, nothing to do; it feels just like being on vacation.

However, I also feel discomfort about the possibility that eventually I will be going back.

How will I feel when I return?

How will I spend my days?

How will I avoid returning to a life of busyness?

What do I fear?

I fear a slow mental death.

I fear an empty life.

I fear having days with nothing to do.

I need to relax. Free time may seem frightening, but it will open my life to new opportunities and bring me to a place yet unknown.

I need to have trust and faith.

I can't wait to see Paul. We've been good friends for many years. (I don't want to think how many it is!)

Paul lives in France and is ahead of me. He quit work several years ago and has been studying psychology, which is one of his multiple passions. He lives in a small village in Alsace in the east of France. It's a piece of paradise in a medieval village, full of flowers, surrounded by vineyards and the Vosges Mountains.

Going there is like going back in time. Life seems so simple there. It's so healthy and much more humane than our busy cities.

But we will not be staying there, as we're going to hike for a week in the Vosges Mountains. We plan to follow trails travelling north, staying in hotels or farms along the way. The area is a hiker's dream, with numerous trails, lakes, streams, rolling hills and deep valleys. Farmers open their doors and provide food and accommodation to visitors. History is alive here, from the prehistoric time to the recent wars.

I must have slept. It is now sunny and bright outside and we will land shortly. As we approach Frankfurt, the landscape looks colourful and inviting. It's amazing to see cars on the Autobahn driving faster than the plane.

Welcome to Frankfurt!

Welcome to Europe!

Welcome to a new life!

- **Do not be afraid of change.**
- **You are responsible for your life.**

Slow down and enjoy life. It's not only the scenery you miss by going too fast. You also miss the sense of where you are going and why.
Eddie Cantor

Twenty years from now, you will be more disappointed by the things that you didn't do than by the ones you did do. So throw off the bowlines. Sail away from the safe harbor. Catch the trade winds in your sails. Explore. Dream. Discover.
 Mark Twain

Nothing happens until something moves.
Einstein

The violets in the mountains have broken the rocks.
Message seen in front of a church in Boston

There is a time for everything, a season for every activity under heaven.
Ecclesiastes 3:1

FITNESS

It is exercise alone that supports the spirit, and keeps the mind in vigor.
Marcus Tullius Cicero

2

This is our first morning!

We had a late evening enjoying a cheese fondue with time to catch up on the latest news - Paul's and mine.

The jet lag took hold of me this morning and I had difficulty getting up. Our shoes and clothes are clean and gleaming. My backpack is well organized. I'm ready to get my shoes muddied, my clothes torn and my backpack messy.

I'm ready to live life to the fullest!

"Now, Michael, are you ready for our big hike, from sunrise to sunset?" asks Paul.

"I'm ready!" I reply. "However, I'm not sure I want to hike all day. I'd like to take time to enjoy the moment, as my mind needs as much a vacation as my body. I'm in good shape, but I don't want to feel rushed and under pressure."

"Are you still running to keep fit?" asks Paul.

"Yes, I keep fit that way. I still run several times a week, but I don't just do that anymore. I swim or bike as well. It's better for my body and it's more balanced. What about you, Paul, what do you do to keep fit?"

"My main activity is walking," replies Paul. "It is what I do most of the time. It's my mode of transportation, and when I have to go a longer distance, I take my bike. Of course, I hike most weekends, as it's really my passion and the perfect activity for me: adventure, exercise, time alone or with people, and time to connect with nature. It's always different, always changing."

"That's great," I reply. "The outdoors is your gym and **exercise is part of your life**."

I lift my backpack and evaluate its weight with some concern. Paul is relaxed, ready to get going, and he does not pay attention to my concern about my backpack. He seems more interested in our discussion.

"Since I exercise on a regular basis, I've noticed lots of changes in my life and not only in my body. I have more energy, more strength, but I think the biggest change is in my mind. **My mind is more relaxed, more positive.** I've slowed down and I enjoy the present moment more intensely. I've noticed that my life has started to change, too. I'm more in control of it and more active. I think the mental benefits of exercising keep me going more than the physical benefits."

"Yes," I reply, "I noticed that as well. My mind is more satisfied. My life is more real and more authentic. Exercise has been a good teacher. I learned to respect my body and be grateful for it. And that brought me to a more complete understanding of what fitness is."

"Tell me about it!" says Paul, while putting on his shoes.

"Most of us associate fitness with aerobic exercise," I explain. "However, if we limit exercise to aerobic activities only, we'll miss other important aspects of fitness."

"Like what?" Paul seems puzzled.

"**Flexibility,** for a start, is an important component of fitness that needs to be developed. I learned that the hard way. I was paying more attention to running than stretching and I started to develop muscle stiffness, especially in the morning. This was affecting my running, and even my daily activities. It got to the point where I had to stop running due to multiple injuries. I finally started to focus on stretching and even started some yoga, a great exercise for a stiff body. The stiffness slowly left me, my mobility improved, and the pain disappeared. I even got rid of the back pain that bothered me for a long time!"

"Yoga, I never thought it would improve flexibility," Paul replies.

"Yes, it's great and, like any exercise, it helps the mind and the body. Pilates is also great for flexibility and for core strengthening. **Balance** is also a crucial element of fitness. It's important to prevent falls and injury."

"What about weightlifting? Is it part of fitness?" Paul asks.

"Yes, as we age, **strength training** is important. Otherwise, our muscles weaken slowly. If you are like me, my lower body is strong, but my upper body doesn't get much exercise. It gets weaker all the time. I need to pay more attention to this."

"Lots to do," agrees Paul, "This is so important! So many people become weaker and more frail as they age. They attribute it to aging, but all of this can be avoided with a little bit of activity."

Our taxi pulls up and we quickly grab our bags, and try to fit them all into the little trunk of the vehicle. This will be our last car ride for a while. We head to the beginning of the trail. Body and mind are ready. The weather is perfect. Sunny and cold in the morning, warm in the afternoon.

Adventure...here we come!

- **The benefits of exercise/physical fitness are numerous, not only for the body, but also for the mind.**
- **Exercise is the foundation of mental health.**
- **If you want control in your life, if you want to slow down, and improve your life, the first thing to do is engage in regular exercise.**

PRACTICE

- The first aspect of physical fitness **is aerobic exercise,** cardiovascular fitness or endurance exercise.

    These activities help your heart, lungs and circulatory system to stay healthy and give you more energy. You don't have to run. You don't have to suffer! A walk three times a week for 30 minutes is all you need. You may want to increase the duration or frequency. You need to diversify your activities to reduce the risk of injury and decrease boredom. Exercises that will help your cardiovascular fitness are:

walking	cycling
running	skating
swimming	cross-country skiing

Other aspects of fitness to develop:

- **Flexibility.** It is the most undervalued component of conditioning. It's essential to prevent injuries and back pain and will help you to move easily. Stretching exercises, yoga and Pilates are good to help develop flexibility. Physiotherapists and athletic therapists are useful professionals to help you develop a program in this area.
- **Strength activities.** If we don't use our muscles, we lose them. Our unused muscles are prone to pain, fatigue and injury. Strong muscles burn calories more easily, give us more energy and strength, and help to prevent diseases like osteoporosis.

    Strength activities are those that make your muscles work against some kind of resistance.

    Examples of strength activities include:
    -heavy yardwork
    -raking and carrying leaves
    -strength training exercises
- **Balance.** It is a basic skill useful to all. If untrained, we progressively lose our sense of balance (proprioception) and increase the risk of falls and injury (especially ankle sprain). The simplest way to develop balance is to stand on one foot while brushing your teeth, and alternate between feet. If it's too easy, do it with your eyes closed, but make sure you don't fall!

If it weren't for the fact that the TV set and the refrigerator are so far apart, some of us wouldn't get any exercise at all.
Joey Adams

Those who think they have no time for bodily exercise will sooner or later have to find time for illness.
Edward Stanley

Lack of activity destroys the good condition of every human being, while movement and methodical physical exercise save it and preserve it.
Plato

A vigorous five-mile walk will do more good for an unhappy but otherwise healthy adult than all the medicine and psychology in the world.
Paul Dudley White

Methinks that the moment my legs begin to move, my thoughts begin to flow.
Henry David Thoreau

FIRST STEPS: BREATHING

When the breath wanders, the mind also is unsteady. But when the breath is calmed, the mind too will be still.
Svatmarama

3

Finally, we are here at the start of the trail. As the taxi leaves us in the middle of the wilderness, I have a strong feeling of freedom and peace. I will have several days without a phone, specific plans or goals.

All I need is in my backpack. All I have to do is follow this trail and find a place to sleep tonight. That's it! It feels so unreal and liberating, so foreign to my daily life. My mind is free. I am not bombarded with multiple messages. I don't have to be time efficient; I don't have to produce anything. And with this freedom comes joy, as I adjust my backpack and slowly climb in the shade and peace of the forest.

Paul breaks the silence.

> "I'm glad to hear that you made the change and decided to quit what you were doing." Paul wonders. "What pushed you to do it so suddenly? The last time I talked to you, you thought you would do it in five to 10 years, so this seems quite sudden!"

> "Well, Paul, many things helped me make up my mind. Getting older was an important factor, since it was somewhat presumptuous of me to assume that I would be alive or healthy 10 years from now. **The present moment is the only thing that I have.** I could have continued what I was doing for 20 years or more, but at the end of each day, I felt drained. My work was swallowing the rest of my life. That I didn't want!"

"Great to have such insight!" replies Paul. "I reached this decision a bit earlier. I couldn't compromise myself any more by doing a job that had lost its appeal to me."

"Yes, and seeing you change work helped me make my decision. But, at the same time, I was struggling with all the excitement of having a fast life - of being busy and successful. One good thing, though, neither of us got into consumerism. It's great **to be free of the tyranny of debt and materialism**. There is a time for everything. Now is the time to find myself again."

"What do you mean, Michael, by finding yourself? Do you mean you got lost?"

"That's certainly the way I feel and I don't really understand it. It's true. I somehow lost myself along the way. I think it happened progressively and I didn't realize it. I'm doing many things now that I wouldn't have done 30 years ago. I feel like I'm on a treadmill - running non-stop, with no time to rest and even no time to wonder where or why I'm running! My mind is constantly on the go. My body is restless, and I need to be busy all the time. Free time frightens me and I have avoided it as much as possible."

The trail rises swiftly and puts an end to our conversation. We are climbing in a pine forest, following several waterfalls and switchbacks. The pines soar toward the sky. Their branches block the sun. It is damp and musty. Nothing else grows here. We arrive at a wooden bridge over a creek and the fresh water is welcome.

"Time to stop and catch our breath!" Paul removes his pack with obvious relief.

"Great! This water looks so inviting! By the way, why do we say 'catch our breath'?"

"No idea. But it's such a good feeling to breathe. I feel like I'm cleaning my body. I like the idea of bringing fresh, pure air into my lungs, my blood, my muscles, and my brain!"

"It's too bad it's not the same when we're stressed. It's more the opposite: the more pressure, the less we breathe. I wonder if it's the same for you, Paul?"

"Yes, and this is one of the reasons I got out of control so quickly. In my hyperactive life, I used to think that speed was the key to success. I didn't even feel or know what I was doing; I was just reacting!"

"Well, Paul, how do you do it otherwise? In my day at work, I don't have time to focus on my reactions or myself. I don't even think about this. My mind isn't functioning that way. Everything is fast and I'm an expert at it!"

"You are an expert at living fast, Michael? I didn't know! Unfortunately, this is the way we're all becoming now, but I don't think this is the right way. There are other ways to live."

"Other ways? Like what? Tell me about them."

"Slowing down is better than speed," explains Paul. "You don't notice the flowers at the side of the road, if you are driving at 200 km/hr. Speed gives you a distorted view of the world."

"I agree, but how do you slow down? I've read all kinds of books about it. I like the idea of slowing down but it doesn't work for me. Oh, it may work for a few minutes, but before I know it, I'm back in the same fast lane. There must be a way to put on the brakes. But I don't know what it is."

"Michael, I've discovered that this is not something we find. **This is something we train for** and I realize that, like every other type of training, it takes time. We need to start slowly. Imagine that somebody wants you to run to become fit, and the first thing he tells you is to run daily for one hour! Chances are, you will end up discouraged, and likely quit before long!

It's the same for the mind.

We don't start by doing long and difficult things.

We need to **start small** and build up progressively.

We need to stay **consistent**, as it takes time to make changes.

The changes we make need to become part of ourselves. If we quit too soon, all will be forgotten quickly. And one of the best and simplest things that I have learned to help me to slow down is breathing."

Paul stretches and spreads his arms wide in front of him. "Ah, stretching feels so good! But you're right, Michael. When I'm under stress, I get tight muscles, my chest doesn't move, and I hardly breathe! The best thing is to do the opposite and take a deep breath.

Try it now.

Close your eyes.

Take a deep, long breath in.

If you slowly count to four while you inhale, it will help you slow down.

Then, pause briefly, and slowly exhale.

Pause again and continue the cycle.

Inhale 1-2-3-4, pause, 1-2-3-4, exhale, pause. Keep your breathing smooth and regular, and breathe with the abdomen. Repeat five times, taking five deep breaths very slowly."

I close my eyes and follow Paul's advice, taking deep breaths slowly, deeply, and the world around me seems to slow down. Somehow, I become more aware of my surroundings: birds singing, wind blowing on my face, the warmth of the sun and the silence.

Paul asks, "Now, tell me what is happening. What do you feel?"

I try to describe my experience. "Everything is slowing down around me and becoming more real. I hear and feel things that I didn't notice before. I am more aware of my body. I usually don't pay attention to my body. And it's strange to feel my body, my chest, lungs and my legs. I'm more in the present, more alive and somehow more part of the world around me."

"I have a similar experience myself," says Paul. "But the more I do it, the deeper it becomes. Taking deep breaths has become the most important thing I've learned. It's more and more a part of my life and it has had a profound positive impact on me. Regular, daily practice is changing my life; I'm more relaxed and don't react as quickly as before in stressful moments. I live more in the present. My days are more enjoyable. I incorporate this in my daily life, doing it three times a day. Sometimes I do it when I have nothing to do, when I am stopped at a red light or waiting in line, or when I feel nervous and anxious. It's fast and easy and I get immediate results. I need some pauses like that in my life to counteract the effect of living at a fast pace. So let's practise this during our time together."

"I like that." I exclaim. "Let's share our experiences. I'd really like to learn something very practical and simple during our time together that I can incorporate into my life. I've heard or read so many complicated pieces of advice that are impossible to follow or remember." I take a few deep breaths.

21

"I like this deep breathing! It is very simple, I can do it anywhere, anytime, and breathing is something I already do. I just need to do it better, on a regular basis, and be more conscious of it."

"Good idea. But it's time to go, Michael, we still have a long walk before we find a place to sleep tonight."

- **Slow down.**
- **Breathing is the first step to slowing down.**
- **Breathe, breathe, breathe.**

PRACTICE

Do deep breathing at least three times a day:
When getting up in the morning
When going to bed
Once in the middle of the day

Practise daily, forever.
Keep reminders in different spots such as your calendar, agenda, and car. Practise wherever you are: at a red light, while waiting in line, while reading, and when under stress.

A healthy mind has an easy breath.
Author unknown

Fear less, hope more; eat less, chew more; whine less, breathe more; talk less, say more; hate less, love more; and all good things are yours.
Swedish proverb

For breath is life, and if you breathe well, you will live long on earth.
Sanskrit proverb.

There is more to life than increasing its speed.
Mahatma Gandhi

Muddied water when left to stand will become clear.
Lao-Tse

Breath is Spirit. The act of breathing is Living.
Author unknown

Focussing on the act of breathing clears the mind of all distractions and clears our energy, enabling us to better connect with the Spirit within.
Author unknown

THE BEGINNING OF MINDFULNESS

There is no enlightenment outside of daily life.
Thich Nhat Hanh

4

The trail continues upwards. The forest is thick, dark and mysterious, yet the freshness and humidity help cool us off.

Suddenly, we are in an explosion of light. The sun is warm. Everything is bright. We arrive at a little lake named Etang du Petit-Haut - a splash of blue in a forest of green. The lake is not large, but it's such a welcome sight after the darkness and humidity of the woods. It's impossible to continue. Time to remove packs and shoes. I step into the water up to my knees.

> "Ah, this water feels so good to my feet, I almost feel like taking a dive in it."

> "I'm starving! Time to eat." says Paul. "By the way, Michael, did you have a chance to practise deep breathing this morning? Any new insights?"

> "I did. But everything is very peaceful now, therefore the effects less dramatic. Under stress in my busy life, I can see how powerful and effective deep breathing would be. I just need to remember to do it! But this is the problem: in times of stress, breathing would not be on my mind. In fact it would be the last thing I would think of!"

> "This is why we need to do it all the time, in times of peace and in time of stress. We need to **practise daily**. So it becomes a routine - part of our life, part of us. It has to be something we do without thinking."

> "It's worth a try." I'm not feeling convinced.

"Before we eat, I'd like you to experience something else, something that will also help you slow down and be more mindful of the present." Paul reaches inside his pack and brings out a baguette that we bought this morning. "Take a small piece of this French bread in your hand.
Just look at it.
Take your time. Have a good look at it.
Now, put it in your mouth and eat it slowly.
Focus completely on the experience of eating this piece of bread: the taste, the texture, the feeling of it in your mouth.
Don't rush it, stay with the taste, with the feeling of eating."

Despite my hunger, I reach for the piece of bread, look at it and slowly put it in my mouth, focusing on the process. "Wow, I never realized that there was so much taste in such a small piece of bread. In all truth, I've never eaten anything like this."

"Yes, quite different from fast food! I've always believed that the act of eating too fast leaves us dissatisfied. We don't really taste what we eat. We are just swallowing air. When I pay attention to what I eat, I enjoy food more. It even tastes different."

"It's really developing awareness of the present. Such a difficult task for a Westerner!" I say.

Paul reaches for more bread, prepares himself a sandwich, and continues the conversation. "We get lost so quickly in our busyness. We've lost all awareness of what we are doing. We lead a life where we are not even alive. We're either on autopilot all day or living in the past or the future."

"But how do you get away from that? It seems so simple and at the same time so difficult to do."

"Again, we need to **start small** and **acquire new habits**," replies Paul. "We need to make a conscious effort to be mindful at a specific time in our day. A good time is just before a meal. It doesn't take extra time out of our day and it benefits us right away. Instead of a fast food mentality, I value and enjoy more of what I eat. Stopping to be thankful before a meal is actually a good way to develop mindfulness and decrease the speed of our lives. By learning to appreciate the little pleasures of life, you can actually increase your level of happiness and decrease depression."

We're back in the forest now, away from the creek and cascades. All is silent except for the occasional bird singing. We're still climbing, but it's getting easier, the summit must be near. I've been thinking of what we discussed at lunch. How will I ever master this skill of slowing down? Paul, guessing my thoughts, gives me more reasons to incorporate this into my life.

"You know this habit of focusing on what I eat or what I do not only helps me to stay in the present, but also helps me to develop gratitude. Instead of focusing on what I don't have, I focus on what I have. And I realize that I have plenty."

As we come out of the forest, we are in the light and the heat. We are at the summit, the Ballon d'Alsace, 1254 meters above sea level. Summits here are called "ballon" because of their rounded tops.

It's time to stop and admire the view. We're at the convergence of three different areas: Alsace, Lorraine and Franche-Comté. We can see villages down in the valley to the north, so far away. Houses are nestled around the church as if seeking protection. Toward the south, the fog hides the valley. A lake is visible down below and looks like a giant drop of water. Farther to the south, over the fog, we see the white summits of the Alps.

"Let's remember to practise our breathing," Paul reminds me.

"Actually, I did practise on my way up. My mind was unsettled for awhile, some habits from my past, so I started taking deep breaths. I became aware of the tension in my body and I was able to relax and return to the present moment. Before doing that, I could have been anywhere, at work or even in the subway. After taking a few deep breaths, I returned to the present, to where I was and what I was doing. I was on the path, one step at a time, and I became completely aware of the process of walking. I was just in the moment, in my steps, in my walk. Nothing else existed. That was really good and completely new to me; I really enjoyed the experience."

- **Slow down and breathe.**
- **Mindfulness makes you present and gives fullness to your life.**
- **Stop and enjoy the little pleasures of daily life.**

PRACTICE

- Breathe as before.
- Before a meal, stop, look, and take your time with the first bite. Focus on the taste and texture, and don't rush.
- Become conscious of two ordinary activities a day, such as taking a shower or drinking a glass of water. Pay attention to them. Stay mindful during the experience.

If we could see the miracle of a single flower clearly, our whole life would change.
Buddha

It's the little moments, that make life big.
Author unknown

True life is lived when tiny changes occur.
Leo Tolstoy

Therefore, do not worry about tomorrow, for tomorrow will worry about itself. Each day has enough troubles of its own.
Matthew 6:24

The present is never our goal: the past and present are our means, the future alone is our goal. Thus, we never live but we hope to live; and always hoping to be happy, it is inevitable that we will never be so.
Blaise Pascal

AWARENESS OF BODY FEELINGS

The body never lies.
Martha Graham

5

I must have fallen asleep; all is quiet. The silence is heightened by a cricket in the distance and the humming of bugs.

It is hot.

I don't feel like moving. The scenery is endless, with deep valleys, small villages hidden among the trees and far away the sudden flatness of the plain. Cities and highways are barely noticeable in the distance. That is where the rest of the world is, fast and busy. So far away, like another planet.

The outline of the trail is easy to see from here.

We are following the old French-German border and the markers are still here. We are using the famous GR 5. GR stands for Grande Randonnee, meaning long-distance hiking trails. Many GR trails criss-cross the country in every direction, marked by red and white signs along the way. The GR 5 is one of the oldest, and goes from Amsterdam to Nice in the south of France, from the North Sea to the Mediterranean Sea.

We overlook lakes in the valley. At times, I feel like I am flying, as the trail crosses over very steep areas. We climb for a while until we reach a summit and come down again; we continue going up and down, mostly in the forest now.

And I breathe. Staying aware of my breathing, staying aware of the present moment. I feel completely in the present. I feel completely part of the forest and nature around me. My mind wanders. I'm in a different world. It's slow and peaceful. The mind works differently here. I think of Henry Thoreau's statement, "*The moment my legs begin to move, my thoughts begin to flow*". It is a flow of thoughts that is effortless - without constraint - free flowing and easy.

Fatigue draws my awareness to my body, my sore back and shoulders and my tired legs.

"I'm getting tired; my body is telling me to stop!" I say.

"That's a good feeling!" Paul replies, somewhat insensitively. "I know that sounds weird, but I have learned that it's important to be aware of our body feelings."

"Why is it important to be aware of our body feelings?"

"Our body is giving us a message, and being aware of our body is valuable. We too often ignore what our body is telling us."

"I agree with you. On a busy day, I completely ignore my body and often don't even realize that I'm tired!"

"I try not to ignore my body," says Paul. "**Awareness of the tension in my body gives me information on what is happening in the present** and helps me to be in touch with my feelings. I've learned to scan my whole body on a regular basis, checking for muscle tension, pain, fatigue, and restlessness. I usually do this after taking a few deep breaths. I became aware, for example, that in times of stress, I get muscular tension in my forehead. This tension comes even if I am not aware that I am experiencing stress. So now, when I feel tension in my forehead, I know that I'm under stress, and by being aware of this, I'm able to deal with it sooner. I just stop, take some deep breaths, and relax my muscles and my mind. I may just stop there or I may explore further and ask myself some questions. What kind of feelings do I have? What is going on in my mind?"

"I never thought about it. For me, body feelings, negative body feelings, are just a nuisance, something to ignore, almost a sign of weakness."

"On the contrary," says Paul, "I've noticed some very positive effects of focusing on the body. Sometimes, I realize my face is tense, my mouth is tight, and my jaw is clenched. If I focus on this, I realize this facial tension is affecting my feelings. If I relax my face, smile, even if I don't feel like it, my mood improves instantly. It feels like the sun coming out of dark clouds. Try it sometime. It's amazing!"

"I'm glad you talked about the body, Paul. I discount it too much and too often separate the mind and the body."

The trail suddenly opens into the light. We're on top of a cliff. There is a lake in the valley below, gleaming in the sun. Being so high up makes me feel like a bird. This lake is called Lac des Perches. It is also called Stern See, meaning Star Lake, due to its sinister legend: a little boy thought a flying star fell into the lake and tried to catch it. He fell into the lake and drowned.

It's getting dark as we arrive at our destination. We'll stay in a small hotel located in the Rouge Gazon, (Red Grass). The name comes from a violent battle that took place here during the seventeenth century - another disturbing story about this beautiful valley

- **Stay in touch with your body and its feelings.**
- **Body feelings are a clue to what is happening in the present.**
- **Body feelings are a clue to what is happening in the mind.**

PRACTICE

- Scan your body fully at least once a day, starting with your face, and going down the rest of the body. Identify what's happening in your body. What kinds of sensations are you experiencing? Don't try to change anything initially. Just observe what is there, and stay with the feelings in the body.
- If you notice tension, practise **progressive muscle relaxation**. It was developed by Dr. Edmund Jacobson to relieve anxiety and stress. Muscles will relax when you first tense them for a few seconds and then release them quickly. Go to the Internet site, *The Technique of Progressive Muscle Relaxation by Dr. Edmund Jacobson,* to read more about it. Briefly, it consists of two phases.

  First phase: contraction of a muscle group for about 10 seconds.

  Second phase: sudden relaxation of the same muscle group for about 20 seconds. Move on progressively to all the muscle groups of your body. If muscles are particularly tense, you may want to repeat the exercise in the various muscle areas more than once.

Those who do not find time to exercise will have to find time for illness.
Old proverb

Our bodies are our gardens - our wills are our gardeners.
William Shakespeare

Sometimes, your body is smarter than you are.
Author unknown

GRATITUDE

To educate yourself for the feeling of gratitude means to take nothing for granted.
Albert Schweitzer

6

The light has a special texture this morning, yellow and soft, surrounded by dark, deep shadows. Everywhere the birds are celebrating the awakening of the sun. The morning freshness has washed away yesterday's heat. What joy, harmony and peace!

Nature is confident and joyful in the new day. This verse comes to my mind: **This is the day the Lord has made, let us rejoice and be glad in it, (Psalms 118:24).** All creation is singing this hymn.

Almost all creation sings. We humans can wake up grouchy, irritable, and overwhelmed by a day that has not yet started.

There is so much beauty, so much peace and so much joy in a morning. I close my eyes and take a deep breath. For a moment, I feel part of the creation and part of the celebration. If only I could sing like those birds.

But the present is so fleeting. My mind moves to the future. I wonder if Paul is awake. Maybe he's waiting for me to have breakfast. I wonder what time it is.

Why is my mind jumping back and forth, first to the future and then to the past? Why does my mind want to leave this perfect moment?

I hope this trip will answer some of these questions and help me change some of my ways.

I realize it will take a long time to retrain my mind and change bad habits.

But now all is peaceful and quiet. Going back to the Bible verse makes me realize the importance of today. Today is special and unique. This day was created, and it's up to me to make it precious and important.

It's good to celebrate the beginning of the day with breakfast. Judging by the size of Paul's plate, there is a lot of celebrating going on!

"Good morning, Paul! This morning I was up early. I went outside and I was touched by all the beauty and peace around me. I feel so grateful to be here, to be alive and to be part of this morning celebration."

"Yes, morning is special," Paul replies. "This is the best time of the day; all is fresh and full of promises. Too often, I take my day for granted, like something owed to me, or worse, sometimes like a punishment. I feel like I'm a spoiled kid. Not satisfied with what I have, constantly expecting and requesting more."

"This is so true. It's only when we lose what we have that we realize how precious it was. Can one learn to be grateful?" I wonder. "I've tried many times to have a gratitude journal. Daily I would write five things I was grateful for. It helped me at the beginning and really improved my outlook on life. But after a few days or weeks it was all gone and I stopped doing it. If I kept doing it, it seemed to lose its meaning. It would be months before I'd go back to it."

"That's interesting, because I just read a study that addressed that question specifically. When practised on a daily basis, gratitude loses its power, possibly due to boredom. If you practise gratitude only once per week, it keeps its power and its positive effect on your life."

"You mean doing the same thing weekly instead of daily? How will I remember to do it on a weekly basis?"

"The best way to remember is to **dedicate a specific day of the week to gratitude**," replies Paul. "By having a special day dedicated to gratitude, you never forget. I've made Monday my gratitude day. It's usually a miserable day for most people. I purposely focus my mind on all the good things happening in my day. Even on bad days I'm always surprised at how many good things are still happening when I look for them."

"Like what? Can you tell me?" I ask.

"Even on a bad day, I have a lot. I'm healthy, I have a job, I have food, I'm happily married, I have a great relationship with my children, I have good friends, and I live in a safe and free country. I could go on and on. Once I start, the flow doesn't stop. I read somewhere that if you have a pair of shoes, a roof over your head and food on your table, you belong to the richest two per cent of the population! The number may not be exact, but it really gives me a perspective on how spoiled I am and how precious all that I have is."

- **Develop an attitude of gratitude.**
- **Gratitude is an antidote to negative emotions.**
- **Gratitude helps us to cope with stress and with Monday mornings!**
- **Gratitude bolsters self-esteem.**

PRACTICE

- Practise gratitude:
  Buy a blank journal/notebook.
  Write down five things for which you are grateful. Do this daily for 21 days (you need that length of time to acquire a new habit), and then do it once per week.
  Start the day by reading a positive saying, and keep reading it during the day. Memorize it.
  Begin your morning in a positive way. See what is good in it, what you will learn and what you will bring to the world. Focus only on the good things.
  Review your day in the evening and pay attention only to the positive things that happened.
- In difficult times, continue to practise gratitude, but instead of doing it weekly, go back to doing it daily.
- Occasionally, read your gratitude journal and be grateful for all the wonderful things you have experienced and accomplished.

Let the heavens rejoice, let the earth be glad;
Let the sea resound, and all that is in it;
Let the fields be jubilant, and everything in them;
Then all the trees of the forest will sing for joy.
Psalms 97:11-12

Let us rise up and be thankful, for if we didn't learn a lot today,
at least we learned a little, and if we didn't learn a little, at least
we didn't get sick, and if we got sick, at least we didn't die; so let
us all be thankful.
Buddha

If the only prayer you said in your whole life was "thank you" that
would suffice.
Meister Eckhart

He is a wise man who does not grieve for the things which he has
not, but rejoices for the thing which he has.
Epictetus

Who does not thank for little, will not thank for much.
Estonian proverb

When eating bamboo sprouts, remember the man who planted
them.
Chinese proverb

Wake at dawn with a winged heart and give thanks for another
day of loving.
Kahlil Gibran

Rather than complain about the thorns of the roses,
Be thankful for roses among the thorns.
Anonymous

ATTITUDE

I have learned the secret of being content
in any and every situation…
Philippians 4:11

7

The morning's freshness is still lingering in the depth of the forest. We've been climbing steadily for awhile. We are silent, lost in our thoughts and in the peace around us. I'm not even sure if I'm thinking. All feels slow and peaceful. Nothing seems more important than the present moment. We just walk, no specific goal in mind, no spectacular accomplishment to be achieved. **We are living in the present**. Past and future are gone.

Nature is seeping into my lungs, my skin, and my whole body. The sun plays with the leaves, their shadows dappling the path. The birds and the wind sing the joy of being alive. Our steps add rhythm to this concert like an ode to the present.

> Now, when did I ever feel like this in my
> previous life?
> I have never had such strong feelings!
> I have never had such a strong feeling of
> being present!
> I have never had such a strong feeling of
> being part of the universe and creation!
> It seems so comical to imagine rushing to
> catch a bus.
> Rushing seems so strange.

The forest suddenly opens onto pastures. We are in the light and sunshine. The trees no longer limit our view and the fields lead to deep valleys. Wildflowers are everywhere and we hear the most melodious song of all - the cow bells, clear, joyful and magical!

You close your eyes,
And you want to hug it all,
You can't stop being grateful.

> You have to stand still,
> You have to be silent,
> And keep looking,

And feeling,
And listening.
Thanks to the Creator!
How majestic are Your ways!
In the valley below, church bells are singing, brought to us by the light breeze.
In my body, my heart, too, is singing.
We're sitting among the flowers, lost in time. But the idea of a farmer's delicious lunch helps get us moving. Many farmers (called marcaires) offer meals and often accommodation. We will enjoy their local products of cheese, smoked meats and home-cooked meals. The view of the tables outside the farm is a welcome sight. Then we see the sign: Closed for the week. Annual vacation.

Bad luck. We didn't realize that farmers took vacations!

"There is another farm 30 minutes away." Paul reassures me.

At a distance, the next farm looks like a dot on the green pasture. It faces the valley, and as we approach we feel a sense of peace, and for good reason: the farm is closed for the day.

Our beautiful plan for lunch has evaporated, and there are no more farms for a long time.

We have to explore the bottom of our backpacks to find some food: yesterday's bread, cereal bars, and a few apples.

"That really is too bad. I've been looking forward to this all morning!" This is the first time Paul has heard me complain.

"Yes, that's too bad," Paul commiserates, still searching for some food at the bottom of his backpack. Then he leans forward and points to the valley. "But at the same time, look! We have the most beautiful view: fields of flowers, cows slowly wandering about, mountains, blue sky and the sun. What else do we need?"

"You're right. I react this way so often. Little disappointments upset me and those inconveniences seem to ruin my life."

"Yes, that's so easy to do! Why do we naturally react in such a negative way? We need to develop an **accepting attitude**. Life is full of good and not-so-good things. We have them both. We don't always choose what we get. But we have the choice of how we will respond to those good and bad things. That decision may change our lives."

"This is so true. When I travel in third-world countries, I'm always amazed at the joy the people have. Although they are poor, often unhealthy and facing death, their joy is so great and acceptance of their condition is amazing."

"I'm sure their attitude to life is different," agrees Paul. "You may be in India, in an overcrowded train full of noise and heat, and be grateful. Or you may sit in your beautiful car, with all the bells and whistles, and feel miserable at the red light that steals 30 seconds of your time."

"I've just reread the book by Viktor Frankl. Even in a concentration camp, he decided to have the right attitude and see some beauty in the day. If somebody can do that in a concentration camp, then I certainly can do it today. And, again, this is a habit to develop. **What we focus on and think about will grow.** If we focus on lack of things or have negative thoughts, that's what we will receive."

"That's right! But it seems so selfish, all this focus on my body, my feelings, and me. What about helping others? "

Paul slowly gets up, signalling the end of our rest.

"Yes, it may seem selfish, but you can still focus on yourself and at the same time help others. One doesn't exclude the other. If you look at your own life, you have not been focusing on yourself all this time. You had a job where you helped others. Spending time to focus on one's self with the idea of improving and becoming a better person, will

help you to help others. You'll have more energy
to help people and be more effective. Nothing to
do with selfishness!"
The trail takes us down the valley and for the first time we see
vineyards. This is the real beginning of Alsace!
The steeple of Thann's Gothic cathedral in the hazy distance indicates our destination for the day.

> - **Choose your attitude.**
> - **No individual or circumstance can force you into an attitude. You choose.**
> - **Don't blame others for your feelings…it is your own responsibility to choose your response.**

PRACTICE

Focus on how you react to problems and the small irritations of life. Simply noticing your reactions is a crucial step in self-awareness. At this stage, don't try to do anything else.

Answer the questions below in writing. Writing will add power to the exercise. You'll have fun reviewing your answers later by seeing how much you have changed (for the better!).

> -What is your attitude today: when you awake, when you go to work, when you finish work, when you eat, when you are stressed or when you deal with problems?
> -Do you accept the present situation?
> -Do you feel helpless?
> -Do you blame somebody or something for your negative feelings?

Everything can be taken from a man but one thing; the last of the human freedoms - to choose one's attitude in any given set of circumstances, to choose one's own way.
Viktor E. Frankl

Don't let the world around you squeeze you into its own mold.
Romans 12:2

My life is filled with many obstacles. The greatest obstacle is I.
Jack Parr

Turn away from evil. And do well. Seek peace, and pursue it!
Psalm 34

We seldom think of what we have, but always of what we lack.
Arthur Schopenhauer

God made us plain and simple, but we have made ourselves very complicated.
Ecclesiastes 7:29

Whether you think you can, or you can't, you are usually right.
Henry Ford

The pessimist sees difficulty in every opportunity. The optimist sees the opportunity in every difficulty.
Winston Churchill

DEVELOPING HABITS

We are what we repeatedly do. Excellence then, is not an act, but a habit.
Aristotle

8

Thann's cathedral is impressive. We look up, admiring the details of the decor in the entrance depicting scenes from the Bible. The cathedral took 200 years to build, beginning in 1442! Time has stopped here. The present meets the past. This is Alsace, with its history, food and culture - so strong and different from the rest of France.

Today, we have a long hike and a long climb. We will be passing by the battlegrounds of World War I. They're still there, untouched and worth the visit. Later, we will reach the summit of the Vosges, the Grand Ballon, almost 1500 meters high.

We slowly make our way through the city. It's market day, and we wander around the stalls. We can find everything here: clothes, food and crafts, most locally produced. Everybody is friendly. Another morning celebration!

We buy some food...in case we find the next farms closed!

> "I have to say we have been doing well so far, Paul. All this learning about living and being in the present. I want to continue doing that. My only concern is what will happen after this trip? Will I forget it all? How can I prevent myself from forgetting our discussions?"

> "Well, Michael, I think the best way to remember is by **developing good habits,**" says Paul. "You wouldn't go to bed without brushing your teeth. We don't even think about it. It's automatic and carved in our minds. It's the same for the brain. We need to develop habits - habits that become part of our lives, part of our brains. Then, it's no

longer difficult to do or remember. We need to take the time to incorporate this learning into our lives. But it takes a minimum of three weeks to acquire a new habit or change an old one, so it's a long process."

"Three weeks! I may forget even before that!" I feel discouraged.

"You're right, Michael, it's so easy to forget! I realize that the only way to remember is by writing down what I want to do. I use a small notebook and read it on a daily basis."

"Great idea! I find that what we've discussed seems easy and doesn't take much time to do. The problem is to keep doing it. The idea of writing my goals down is good. I'm curious to see what all those little changes will do in my life."

"Yes, by putting our goals in writing, they become clearer and more powerful." Paul agrees, "And it makes it easier to keep practising all that we have discussed. That way they become part of our minds and lives. I have learned that trying to change too many things at once doesn't work. It's better to start slowly. When you look at it, there is a lot we can change, if we keep practicing what we discussed. Think about
exercising,
breathing,
gratitude,
attitude,
focusing on the body,
learning to feel and relax the body."

"And taking the time to eat by focusing on the food and developing mindfulness, the most difficult task for me," I add.

"What has helped me a lot is to memorize some quotes that illustrate what I am working on. I keep repeating them regularly. They become part of my thoughts and change my mind and life over time. Once I've developed a habit, I realize that I still need constant reminders, on a weekly, monthly and even yearly basis. I don't trust my mind! My mind starts cutting corners, and in difficult times, I don't remember anything. It has to be a lifelong habit. **Nothing is finished or acquired forever!**"

"It seems ridiculous, Paul, that I have to learn or relearn such basic things as that. In our modern life, we feel we can do anything. This is such an illusion. We're not even able to get in touch with ourselves. No wonder we have problems with relationships. How can we expect to perform better with others when we don't even do well with ourselves?"

- **Assimilate what you have learned.**
- **Don't move ahead without integrating what you have learned already.**
- **Create reminders of what you need to practise.**
- **It takes several weeks to form a new habit.**

PRACTICE

- Practise what you have learned.
- **Memorize quotes**. Keep the same quote for at least one week. Repeat it many times a day.
- **Don't move too fast**. Don't try to incorporate any other changes until you have assimilated what we have discussed so far. Be patient.
- **Habits to incorporate into your life:**
    Breathing
    Exercise/physical activity
    Mindfulness (start at meal time)
    Gratitude
    Attitude
    Focus on the body's feelings

A nail is driven out by another nail. Habit is overcome by habit.
Desiderius Erasmus

Habits change into character.
Ovid

Powerful indeed is the empire of habits.
Publilus Syrus

First we form habits, and then they form us. Conquer your bad habits or they will conquer you.
Rob Gilbert

The chains of habits are generally too small to be felt until they are too strong to be broken.
Samuel Johnson

Motivation is what gets you started. Habit is what keeps you going.
Jim Ryun

Bad habits are easier to abandon today than tomorrow.
Yiddish proverb

The unfortunate thing about this world is that good habits are so much easier to give up than bad ones.
Somerset Maugham

FEELINGS

It isn't intellect that connects us to other people; it is feeling.
Charles Fowler

9

As we step inside, we know we're in a special place. There are delicious smells of food, smoked meat and coffee. There are noises of laughter, animated voices, and the clatter of dishes.

There is life here! There is joy here!

We've finally made it. We've reached the Molkenrain farm. We're sitting in front of this farmer's beautiful meal: smoked ham, bacon, cheese and country bread, all locally produced. A glass of Riesling adds to the delight. It's a crime to eat quickly. Haste is not welcome here. It stays outside. All around us, we feel joy and gratitude. It is such a good feeling to be here.

But getting here wasn't easy. Clouds and fog suddenly surrounded us at the worst time. We were out of the forest, in the open fields with no landmarks to follow. We couldn't see where we were. No trail or markers! Our vision was limited to a few feet. Drifting the wrong way would have been so easy. Paul's sense of direction helped us to find our way.

> "You know, for a while I really thought we were lost. I was getting worried," Paul says with relief.

> "Me too! I felt something like fear - a very familiar feeling to me. I wonder why I experience negative feelings so strongly and often don't even notice positive feelings?"

> "I don't think I'm that way. I try to avoid my negative feelings by keeping busy." Paul says, sipping his wine.

> "And what's wrong with that? Why do you want to stay with unpleasant feelings?"

"I realized that **feelings, good and bad, are part of life** and that I've spent a large part of my life running away from them. I had the mistaken belief that I could not bear the pain of negative feelings. However, the pain I was trying to escape was already here in me and I couldn't run away from it. I needed to stay with it."

"Why would you want to do that?" I ask surprised.

"Because it's impossible to escape. Feelings will come back in a different way, like anxiety or anger. However, if I stay with them - if I stay with the pain, the fears, and the anxiety and feel them, they're not as painful as I feared. There's something to learn there about myself. Feelings give me a clue to what's going on in my life and in my mind; they're a signal that something needs to be addressed and not ignored. And life is also about pain and suffering and I need to accept this truth. Accepting it helps me to have a better attitude in my day."

I still have difficulty understanding and accepting what Paul is telling me. "Why do I want to be in touch with my negative feelings? Often I don't feel capable of handling them!"

"I don't think it's the feelings that you have difficulty handling, Michael, I think it's the fear of experiencing those negative feelings that scares you. After years of repressing them, you're uncomfortable with them. Relaxing and applying what we talked about earlier will help you face your feelings.
Try it now.
Take a deep breath.
Focus on your body and the tension you are experiencing.
Relax your body.
You may then be ready to focus on

your feelings. You don't have to do anything with them. You don't have to change them. **Feelings are not wrong or right**; they are just there."

"Well, somehow, it doesn't feel right, it feels scary."

"Yes, it's scary to face our pain, and it's scary to do something we're not used to doing. Just tell yourself something like this: I'm safe going into my feelings, and they are not dangerous. It's normal to have painful or negative feelings; nothing bad will happen by staying with my feelings," Paul tells me.

"This is so new to me! The process scares me, but I'll do it. This is the only way to know. But I still wonder why bad feelings are so strong and good feelings seem much more difficult to experience?"

"There may be many reasons for this," concludes Paul. "Positive feelings are sometimes more settled and often we don't identify them as positive feelings. Would you say quietness is a positive feeling? Or peace? The most important thing is to take the time to slow down, to be in touch with ourselves, and our feelings."

- **Feelings are important; they are part of our life experience.**
- **It is important to stay in touch with our feelings.**
- **Avoiding feelings is an illusion, they will come back.**
- **It is important to slow down and take the time to focus on feelings, to really feel them.**

PRACTICE

- Breathe deeply three times.
- Relax your body. Focus on any tension in your body, and release it.
- Focus on your feelings. It's helpful to have a process to identify feelings. The following is one way of doing it. Ask yourself:

    Is it a good or bad feeling?
    Place the feeling into one of the following four core emotions:

      anger,
      sadness,
      joy and
      fear.

    Then it will help to ask questions like:
    Where is this feeling in my body?
    How is my body responding to this feeling?
    Does my feeling have any physical characteristic such as color, shape or size?

- Make a list of good feelings (see Appendix A), read them and try to identify them.

If you focus on your feelings that way, they will become more familiar and clear to you.

When I do well, I feel good. When I do bad , I feel bad. And that's my religion.
Abraham Lincoln

Mankind is governed more by their feelings than by reason.
Samuel Adams

Eyes that do not cry, do not see.
Swedish proverb

Let's not forget that the little emotions are the great captain of our lives and we obey them without realizing it.
Vincent Van Gogh

The feeling is often the deeper truth.
Augustus Hare

We think too much and feel too little.
Charlie Chaplin

STORM

Smooth seas do not make skillful sailors.
African proverb

10

My body does not want to continue. My shoulders are sore from the backpack and my legs are stiff from our daily exercise. However, it's time to leave the comfort of the ferme-auberge (farmhouse inn) and get going. It's no longer foggy outside and the sun is warm as we begin our slow climb.

We arrive at the memorial of the Word War I battlefield. Everything is the same as it was then: trenches, casemates, barbed wire. Eighteen months of fighting and 30, 000 deaths!

We spend time walking around the area. The view is amazing and this is the perfect place to scan the valley. I wonder how I would have felt here during the war with death as my closest companion.

We're climbing again. The trail is pleasant, offering wide views of the valleys and the Plaine d'Alsace which looks flat and busy in the distance. And we finally reach the highest point of the Vosges, the Grand Ballon.

We dominate the world around us and the view is endless. The flat plain ends at the Black Forest. We can see many villages and cities on the plain. I think of an anthill. I feel remote from all that as it is so peaceful here. How can I ever go back and be part of that incessant movement and speed?

Here is peace and silence; I am surrounded by beauty and flowers everywhere.

All of a sudden, clouds cover the sky. What was warm and safe is suddenly cold, wet and threatening. The wind is blowing. It is raining and thundering. It is cold and in spite of our raingear, we are getting wet. Mud and water cover the trail. I can't even see where I am going. I feel like running to escape this. How is it possible for the weather to change so quickly?

"Now, let's stop for a while," says Paul.

"Stop! Are you crazy? I'm wet, cold, tired and I want to get out of here! The last thing I want is to stop and get more of this misery. Let's go! Let's keep going."

"No! Michael, let's stop for a few minutes. It won't be long."

"I'm not sure I like this."

"Just stop and pay attention to your body. What do you feel?"

"What do I feel? Tiredness, cold, tightness in my body, I am certainly not relaxed!"

"Michael, this is the time to focus on your feelings," says Paul. "What are they?"

"I feel scared, tired, vulnerable, and mad at the weather and at you, Paul, for making me stop in the rain! Enough of this, let's get going."

Paul is insistent. "Just a minute! Let's go a little deeper. What are your thoughts at the moment?"

"Paul, that's enough! I don't want to go deeper. I want to get out of this misery!"

"You will, but can you focus on what's happening in your mind at the moment?"

"I'll talk another time. Stay here if you want, Paul. I'm going!"

"Yes, we will be going shortly. Just pay attention to your thoughts at this moment. What are they?"

"I think that the weather is stupid. What's happening isn't fair. It should not be happening. Why

is it raining when I'm hiking? This is my first vacation in a long time and I deserve good weather.
I deserve a good time and this isn't right. I'll get
lost or struck by lightning. I'm so tired. I don't
need this. Get me out of here!"

"Wow, lots of thoughts! I know, Michael, you
want to get going, but just before we go, let's practise what we talked about. Let's close our eyes and
take a deep breath. Let's not focus on the weather. Just focus on the breathing. Slowly, take three
deep breaths in a row. Don't speed up the process.
Slowly. Now let's focus on what is around us: the
rain, the wind, the cold, the fatigue, and the tension in our bodies. What are you experiencing
now? Don't fight it. Just feel it."

The wind is pushing me away from the safety of
the trail. The rain is beating my face, adding to my
misery.

"I feel the cold. The rain is hitting me and the
wind is pushing me. My feet are wet and cold and
I'm tired of being here talking about my feelings.
I want to be in a warm, dry place away from the
wind. So, Paul, for the last time, let's go! Leave
your experiment for another day!"

"You're right; it's time to get moving. We're getting cold. Let's talk about it later."

- **Don't avoid your feelings, even the negative ones. There is a message in them.**
- **There are no good or bad feelings.**
- **It is good to take the time to stop and focus on feelings, especially in difficult times.**

PRACTICE

In difficult times, it is important to remember the following:
>Don't try to fix the problem right away.
>It is important to stop.
>It is important to take deep breaths.
>It is important to connect with your feelings.

In difficult times, everything moves quickly and the first step is to slow down.
>Get in touch with your body.
>Get in touch with your feelings.
>This is not the time to resolve or fix anything. It is the time to become aware of what is and be aware of the present, even if it's painful.

Flow with whatever is happening and let your mind be free. Stay centered by accepting whatever you are doing. This is the ultimate.
Chuang Tzu

Difficult times have helped me to understand better than before, how infinitely rich and beautiful life is in every way, and that so many things that one goes worrying about are of no importance whatsoever.
Isak Dinesen

Pain is inevitable, suffering is optional.
M. Kathleen Casey

In the middle of every difficulty lies opportunity.
Albert Einstein

FEELINGS ARE THE KEY TO THOUGHTS

You have power over your mind - not outside events.
Realize this , and you will find strength.
Marcus Aurelius

11

We were in the rain and the wind for a long time, but we finally reached a warm place. Ah, I am enjoying the pleasure of feeling the heat, the safety of the house, the smell of food and the presence of people. We are warm, we are dry, and we are safe, savouring our meal.

Paul, while enjoying his warm soup, brings the conversation back to our recent misery and suggest we talk about what happened in the storm. How it felt to be there. How it felt to stop and do deep breathing in the middle of the storm.

"I have to admit that doing deep breathing made me a bit more relaxed." I say.

"And what were you experiencing just before doing deep breathing?"

"You know what I was experiencing, Paul! I was miserable, tense, tired, and afraid. I didn't want to stop and focus on my feelings and thoughts. In a situation like that, my mind tells me to escape - to get away from it all as quickly as possible and eliminate the pain. That's really all there was on my mind in those moments. I realize that I was fighting the present. Not accepting it, but trying to escape it. And, I was trying to escape you, Paul, and your idea of focusing on deep breathing. I believe this is typical of the way I behave in difficult times."

"And what happened to you after doing deep breathing?"

I'm not sure I like this conversation. I would rather practise focusing on the meal in front of me, a much more pleasant prospect. "I think doing deep breathing helped me become more aware of my body, my feelings and even my thoughts. It was as if I had two persons or two minds inside me.

One was telling me that it would be good to let go and accept the situation. It would be good to relax and trust my friend Paul, that it would all turn out well and that it was not bad after all. And the other mind was telling me this is terrible! Why am I here? Why is it raining? Why do we have to be in the rain when everybody else is enjoying the comfort of home? Why is Paul forcing me to stay in the rain? We'll never get away from here. We'll get lost, hurt or hit by lightning."

"My experience was similar to yours, Michael, but I wanted to experience the effect of stopping, trying a new way to react and seeing what would happen. This was an opportunity for both of us to grow. I clearly saw **the source of my strong negative feelings: my mind!** My mind was telling me terrible things the same as yours was. And those thoughts gave birth to very negative feelings. And those negative feelings reinforced my mind's beliefs that something was seriously wrong. It became a vicious circle, giving me even more catastrophic thoughts I didn't know how to respond to."

"Yes, it looks like my mind is the cause of a lot of my distress. How could I change that?"

"That's the point of our discussion. The key is to increase our awareness of what we're doing in the present, but we also need to train the mind. In the same way that our mind fools us with bad and catastrophic thoughts, we can also fool our mind with good, positive thoughts. We're the ones in control. **We need to learn to renew and retrain our minds in a positive way.**"

I'm skeptical of this scenario. "It sounds like a lot to do and learn. It sounds so artificial."

"Now, Michael, listen to your mind talking there! Do you see what your mind is telling you?"

I realize that my mind doesn't want to change. My mind seems pleased to be in the negative state. I listen to Paul with interest. "Focusing on the negative events in life amplifies them and affects us deeply in a negative way," he says. "This doesn't sound healthy, but this is exactly what we do! However, **we have a choice.** If we don't train and control the mind, it will lead our lives and the results won't be good. We will expose ourselves to pain, distress, negativity and rigidity."

"I know, I know. You may be right. But it's easy to continue in the same old way. I need to become aware of my thoughts, especially negative, destructive, and unhealthy thoughts. I'm not aware of them most of the time." I confess.

The heat and the food help me appreciate the present and forget our difficult time.

"I often take good things for granted," I add, "and don't even pay attention to the many gifts and special moments I have every day. Precious moments like this one now. Why am I so demanding, so dissatisfied, instead of being happy and thankful for what I have?"

"I think society trains us to be that way," Paul says. "It makes us believe that happiness is consumption and that we should want more all the time - a new car, a bigger house, always more, always in the future. We hear it all the time. Even if we don't believe it, it affects our thoughts and rules our lives. How can we challenge that?"

The storm has passed. All is peaceful, fresh, and renewed. We are not going down to the valley, but staying on top, travelling from summit to summit. There are very few trees and the view is beautiful, endless and always new. Here the Vosges Mountains try to imitate the Alps. They are steep and the slopes disappear off the side of the trail. As we slowly keep going, we meet some cars. A road goes along beside the trail, sometimes very close, sometimes far away. It was built during World War I to provide supplies for the army. Now it supplies tourists to the hotels, a reminder that "civilization" is not far away.

The trail dives suddenly into the valley, no more wind, no more cars, and we arrive at the bottom of the Honeck, the third highest summit. We are in a protected area here. The site is blessed with an abundance of alpine flowers. The trail adds interest by taking us among rocks, cliffs, and precipices. Railings are in place to prevent a fall. Are we in the Alps?

We arrive at our destination, Col de la Schlucht, a pass between Alsace and Lorraine. We're ready to remove our shoes and give our legs some rest. The road is beside us again, and with it, the welcome sight of hotels.

Civilization is good sometimes.

- **Feelings are the key to our thoughts**
- **By being in touch with our feelings, we are able to identify our thoughts.**
- **We need to challenge our negative or destructive thoughts and beliefs.**

PRACTICE

We need to identify our thoughts. Our first clues are:
> Our bodies
> Our feelings.

What is the feeling behind our tense bodies?
What is the thought behind the negative feeling?

It's useful to identify our dysfunctional thoughts.
You will find a full list on the website : www.HealthyMind. com(called cognitive distortions) or in the book *Feeling Good* by David Burns.

A simple way to identify our dysfunctional thoughts is by noticing the use of the following words:
> Should
> Never
> Always
> Have to
> Ought

Those words are a sign of our dysfunctional thoughts and need to be banned from our vocabulary!

The only thing we have to fear is fear itself.
Franklin D. Roosevelt

To know and not to do, is not to know.
Chinese proverb

You can chain me, you can torture me, you can even destroy this body, but you will never imprison my mind.
Mohandas Gandhi

I have simply tried to do what seemed best each day as each day came.
Abraham Lincoln

And do not be conformed to this world, but transformed by the renewing of your mind.
Romans 12:2

Be vigilant, guard your mind against negative thoughts.
Buddha

YOUR MIND AND THOUGHTS ARE NOT YOU

*I'm an old man and have known a great many
troubles, but most of them never happened.*
Mark Twain

12

The area we are in is magical - lakes, deep valleys, legends, and wilderness. There are no roads here. It's another day to enjoy and discover as we climb in the alpine scenery. We have been silent most of the morning, enjoying the fresh morning air, and the scenery. I feel at peace, rested and relaxed. It is nice to be hiking here, feeling and hearing nature around me. Nothing disturbs me. My steps keep me in the present. My mind is quiet, not trying to guess what tomorrow will bring. Is this not the way I need to be all the time?

The trail emerges from the surrounding forest and brings us to the edge of a cliff overlooking Green Lake.

The water beautifully mirrors the surrounding forest. We both stop in awe. Paul finally removes his pack and sits on the ground.

"This is how I feel when I meditate. My mind has been racing all over the place and is finally at peace." he says.

"You talk as if your mind is another person."

"Yes, you are right and I believe it is!" Paul replies. "I used to associate my mind with myself, but **I learned that my mind isn't me.**"

"What do you mean; your mind isn't you?" I find that comment strange. "I don't understand that. My mind is who I am! It leads my life. Why do you say your mind is not you?"

Paul continues, "Let me answer that with a different question. Do you remember when we were in the storm? Your mind was fighting the present, and you were having all kinds of negative thoughts.

Do you think that those thoughts were you?

Do you think those thoughts represented the truth?

You could have reacted differently. You could have taken it as a game, as something new, exciting and positive.

Therefore, exactly who are you, Michael? The first set of thoughts, which are reactive, anxious, focusing on the negative and dramatic?

Or, the second set of thoughts, which are positive, flexible, looking forward to a new challenge and knowing that all would go well in the end?"

This comment hits me like a brick wall. "I like to think I am more like the second set of thoughts, able to deal with difficult situations! But I act more like the first set of thoughts, which are fearful and anxious. Why is that?"

"I believe the main reason is that we identify completely with our thoughts. However, I came to the realization that **my thoughts don't represent reality**. They come from my past, my self-talk and false beliefs and are the result of a distorted perception of reality."

"I'm confused about this new concept, Paul. You need to explain it better."

"Our thoughts are the result of our self-talk (what we say to ourselves about the events in our lives) and false beliefs acquired in the past from our peers or experience. Self-talk and false beliefs are often very difficult to identify, as they've been with us for a long time and they are part of us. We need to become aware of them, examine them, challenge them and, of course, change them, if they don't reflect our values and ourselves or if they have a negative impact on our lives. I see this as renewing the mind."

"Who am I, then, if I'm not my thoughts?" I'm still confused about all this.

"I like to think that I'm the one in control, the one who decides how to act and who takes control of my thought processes. It's me who is able to change the flow and the quality of my thoughts. I am not my thoughts. **I am the decision maker!**"

"Well, Paul, this is difficult for me to comprehend and accept. However, one thing I'm sure of is that I don't like to think that I'm living in a fearful, reactive mode."

"But that's what you did!"

I stretch my legs, feeling uncomfortable with who I am, or with what my mind is. "Yes, I did react in a negative way and that's exactly how I react in difficult times. Why is that?"

Paul seems amused by my reaction. "I'm not sure there is a reason, but that's what happens when your mind is untrained. We're creatures of habit and it's so easy to develop a closed, rigid attitude, living in fear of the present, fear of difficulties and fear of change. The mind becomes rigid, negative, fearful, afraid of new ideas, afraid of pain and afraid of feeling. It's like a slow death. This is when you become old, and it has nothing to do with age."

"Not a very positive picture, but I agree. I've seen many people like this, with no life, no hope, and no spark in their lives. But let's go back to the question of who I am. I'm not too clear about it yet. You tell me I am not my thoughts; I'm more like the decision maker. The decision maker for my reaction to life situations and the decision maker for the type of thoughts I have. Is that right?"

"Yes, that's what I believe, Michael. I found that by believing that, I take more responsibility for my life. I'm the one who decides how I react. This belief has changed my life for the better."

"Seems to me that this would be hard to do - especially when everything's going badly and when I'm under stress!"

Paul reinforces his point. "That's exactly the point. Who are we? Who are you in difficult times? A desperate, negative, passive individual, or somebody in control of his decisions and destiny? We are free to choose."

"It seems so difficult to go against the flow. It feels easy to blame others or events instead of taking charge of my thoughts."

"You're right. Blaming others or events may be easier in the short term, but not in the long term. Every day we have many little decisions to make. If we let go, we will develop a negative or passive attitude. Little by little we will change for the worse and we will eventually see life in a very distorted and negative way!"

"Are you suggesting that we need to train our mind and our thoughts?

"That's right, Michael, and it's not a suggestion. If we don't train and control the mind, it will control us in a negative way. If we mistake our mind for ourselves, we will believe that we are negative and passive; that's the way we are. We won't even try to change. We will accept our mind's dysfunctions as our own. But instead of being our enemy, our mind needs to become our ally, and this will only happen if we train it."

"It all started very simply and felt more like a game. Now I'm not sure this is so simple. I'm not sure I like what I'm hearing. It sounds too difficult!"

Paul assures me this process isn't all that difficult, but that it's a process that will take time. Lots to digest as we continue our journey.

We are finally in a ferme auberge for the night. Before going to sleep, I review my day and all the great things in it: the nice weather, the scenery, the fresh air of the forest, the songs of the birds, and the peacefulness of the day. I'm grateful that our bodies are able to carry us and our backpacks, for the pleasure of physical exercise, the mystery and magic of the lakes, the mountains, the trail, the markers on the trail that prevent us from getting lost, the food and the hospitality on the farms. There is so much to be grateful for as I fall asleep.

- **We are not our thoughts.**
- **We need to train and control our mind.**
- **We are responsible for our state of mind.**

PRACTICE

It's time to **challenge your thoughts, beliefs and the self-talk** behind them.

- One way of doing that is in writing.
- Choose a situation that leads to an unpleasant feeling.
- Are you able to identify the emotion? Describe it.
- Are you able to identify the thoughts or the self-talk that lead to this emotion? What are you telling yourself about the situation?
- How could you respond differently?
- Write a different and positive response to counteract your automatic, negative thoughts.

This needs to be done on a regular basis, daily, at first. The best time to do this is when you are feeling upset, irritable, anxious, depressed, or simply not well.

The only thing some people do is grow older.
Ed Howe

They are able because they think they are able.
Virgil

The mind is its own place, and in itself can make a heaven of Hell,
a hell of Heaven.
John Milton

The will… is the driving force of the mind. If it's injured, the mind
falls to pieces.
August Strindberg

MORE MIND TRAINING: MEDITATION

~~~~~~~

... Meditate in your own hearts upon your bed, and be still.
Psalms 4:4

13

Ah, the joy of coffee! You add French bread, homemade jam and butter, and you have the perfect start to a day!

We are leaving the "wilderness" today to go down to the base of the mountains and see some of those small picturesque villages in Alsace. The way down is easy at first, but the weight of my backpack pushes me down. My legs are beginning to hurt.

"I didn't realize going down would be so tiring." I complain.

"Keep going, we're almost there." Paul reassures me. "The descent isn't very long, and then we'll have a few short climbs before we rest."

I have heard the words "we're almost there" many times and know it could mean a few more minutes, or, more likely, a few more hours. I need to occupy my mind to get away from the fatigue in my legs.

"I've been thinking of what we discussed last night, controlling the mind and our thoughts. I often feel overwhelmed by so many thoughts. It feels like my mind is out of control, all over the place. I don't even have time to pay attention to the type of thoughts I have."

Paul agrees. "You're right; that's very true! I've been trying to control the flow of my thoughts as well and I realize **I need to quiet my mind constantly**. I read somewhere that the mind is like the surface of the ocean, always moving, dependent on the wind and the elements. But the mind needs to be more like the bottom of the ocean, always quiet, peaceful, even if there is a storm at the surface. As we said yesterday, the mind is our worst enemy. We try to focus and our mind wanders off. We try to control our stress, but anxiety keeps us awake at night. We need an ally, not an enemy."

"I like that description. You're right. In periods of stress, my mind is racing, hyperactive and not able to focus well on what's happening. Incessant motion prevents me from dealing with my feelings and my life. Tell me, Paul, how can I quiet my mind? It sounds like such an impossible task."

"Did you notice what your mind said to you right now? If that's your belief, then you're right, you won't be able to slow down and control your mind."

"Okay, Paul, point well taken; but you didn't answer my question. How can I slow down my mind?"

"I believe that the best way to slow the mind down is by doing meditation."

"Meditation? What do you mean?" I ask.

"We all agree that it's good to train the body, but we neglect the most important part of ourselves, the mind and training the mind. **Meditation is one way of training the mind.**"

"Tell me more about it. It sounds a bit weird to me! How do you do it?"

Finally, Paul suggests that we stop. It's good to stretch and rest my legs as I listen to him.

"The first step in meditation is to choose a focus. You need to focus the mind on something. Otherwise, the mind will be all over the place. The most common focus used in meditation is the breath. You **focus on your breathing** and become aware of it. Focus on inhaling; feel the air going through your nose and your lungs and feel your chest expanding. Then, feel the air leave your body and your lungs as you exhale, air coming out of your nose. Try it. Just take a normal breath."

Leaning against a tree, I focus my mind on the air coming into my nose and my chest, and then the air leaving my lungs.

"How did it feel?" Paul asks me after a few minutes.

"Let me see. The feeling is difficult to describe at first. I certainly slowed down, became more aware of my body and my breath. But my mind was still very active. I kept getting all kinds of different thoughts and didn't focus on the breath that much."

Paul says this reaction is normal. "You will have thoughts. They will come. You can't avoid them. Don't fight them. You just need to accept them. Don't get frustrated with them. Have what's called a passive attitude toward your thoughts. Just observe them and keep bringing your mind back gently to the breathing. By doing this, you not only slow down, but you also increase your awareness of the present. You'll train your mind to slow down and focus."

"So that's it? If I keep meditating like that, I'll be able to control my mind?"

"You may, but be careful. You should not have any specific goal while meditating. Having a goal will set you up for failure. Our friend, the mind, will be quick to measure results and get discouraged and helpless if we don't show improvement in the process. There is no good or bad meditation, and sometimes you feel like you're not able to get into it. Don't have any expectations!"

"And how long do I need to do this?"

"Meditate for as long or as short a time as you like. Some people meditate for one hour. I don't know where they find the time! The most common advice is about 20 minutes, but as little as five minutes is fine. Again, it's important to have no specific expectations and it's important to start slowly like everything else. It's better to continue to do five minutes daily than to do 45 minutes and quit after a few days, due to a lack of time."

"And that's it, just focus on the breathing?" It seems too simple to me.

Paul continues, "You can change the focus as you like: a candle, a flower, the feeling of the sun on your face; or you may choose to meditate on gratitude or other feelings."

We are back in "civilization" with roads, cars, houses and people all around. It is nice to see human life and activity here. It still feels peaceful, a good transition from our hike. The town of Eguisheim welcomes us with its cobblestone streets and medieval houses. Flowers are everywhere. Very little has changed since the Middle Ages. Even cars are not found here, as the streets are too narrow.

It is pleasant to wander around the circular streets looking at the old buildings. Everything feels so clean and perfect. It seems unreal to think that people live in such beauty! This is where we'll spend the night. It's difficult not to feel grateful in a place of such harmony.

> - **Slow down the mind and control the flow of thoughts.**
> - **One way of doing this is to practice meditation.**

PRACTICE

- Meditate!
- Set aside some time during the day (5-20 minutes) in a quiet area and practise meditation by focusing on the breathing. You may not be able to do it well or long, but this does not matter, just do it.
- Another good way to meditate is by being completely aware of what you are doing at the time. Focus your mind completely on the task - for example, as you dry dishes. Just look at the dishes, feel them, stay in the present and don't rush the process.
- Running and walking are good ways to meditate. You can focus your mind on the breathing, or on your body exercising, or on the feelings you are experiencing. You'll want to change your feelings if they aren't positive. In our multitasking society, this is a great way to do more than one thing at a time.

Half an hour's meditation each day is essential, except when you are busy. Then a full hour is needed.
St. Frances de Sales

I shut my eyes in order to see.
Paul Gauguin

A mind too active is no mind at all.
Theodore Roethke

Isaac went out to meditate in the field at the evening.
Genesis 24:63

Of the glorious majesty of your honor, of your wondrous works, I will meditate.
Psalms 1

POSITIVE THINKING

Finally, brothers, whatever is true, whatever is noble, whatever is right, whatever is pure, whatever is lovely, whatever is admirable – if anything is excellent and praiseworthy - think about such things.
Philippians 4:8

14

It's breakfast time and the day is full of promise. My body and mind are rested and I'm ready to go. A buffet breakfast awaits us with croissants, yogurt, fruit, smoked ham, honey and, of course fresh, crispy bread.

"It's difficult to feel bad in front of such a feast!" I can't help adding, "**The morning is the best time to set our attitude** for the rest of the day. I read that Norman Vincent Peale starts his day every morning by repeating three times 'This is the day the Lord has made, let us rejoice and be glad in it.' By saying that, it really helps him to see and set his day in a very positive way."

"I like that," Paul says. "I'll have to add this to my morning routine."

"Do you have a morning routine?"

"Yes, most mornings, I do a quick scan of my whole body to see if I have tension anywhere. Sometimes my body is already tense when I wake up. Then I check my feelings, especially if my body is tense. Sometimes I discover anxiety, or irritability, often for no obvious reason. I'm usually able to improve those feelings right away and I don't have to carry them inside me all day. I make a conscious effort to be aware of my body and my feelings several times during the day as well, especially in times of stress. It doesn't take long; it becomes automatic and it's a good habit. I'm able to relax my body right away and become aware of my dysfunctional thoughts."

We leave the beautiful village of Eguisheim. The trail wanders around vineyards and suddenly leads into a forest. I wonder why we don't learn all the things Paul has mentioned in school. It would avoid so much suffering. Imagine, courses in attitude, relationships, and mind training. I think that would get me back to school!

Paul is quiet. He seems concerned about something. We've been walking in this forest for several hours. We haven't seen a marker indicating that we're on the right trail for quite some time. The map doesn't help us, as we don't know where we are. We are lost.

Paul finally admits, "I am not sure which way to go! Should we continue or should we turn around until we find the marked trail again?"

"If we continue, we may become really lost, and have to hike many extra hours to find a place to sleep tonight. But if we turn around, we may go back to the beginning, and I don't really like that either. What's the solution, Paul?"

Paul surprises me with his reply. "In this situation, we don't have a solution. We will never know the right answer. We don't have control of the situation. We're lost and we don't know the right way to get out of the situation. This is reality and we have to accept it. And we also need to accept the consequences of our decision."

We decide to keep going, with the nagging feeling that it may not be the right decision. I look at the trees as we walk, with the hope of seeing a marker.

"When you think of it, Michael, this isn't a big deal. We can look at the situation from a different perspective. Getting lost may be positive, as we may discover a new area or find something unexpected. And getting lost here isn't very serious; villages and farms are everywhere. It will be a good experience; we'll learn something from this. We'll really appreciate finding a place to eat and sleep tonight which we've been taking for granted so far. This may end up being the best memory of the trip!"

I try to have a positive attitude, but I also have feelings I don't like. I try to explore them further to identify the thoughts behind them.

Anger is one of the feelings I'm experiencing, anger at whoever marked the trail and did such a poor job!

I could be angry at Paul. After all, I was following him! If he'd been more careful and paid more attention, we wouldn't be lost. I shouldn't have followed him. I should have been more careful.

Helplessness is another feeling I'm experiencing. My mind tells me that we'll never find the trail. We're really lost and will wander forever. We will be cold and it may even rain, or I may end up breaking a leg on these stupid steep trails.

I'm amazed at the number of negative thoughts I have.

"I'm realizing it's very easy for me to have a negative attitude," I say. "And whatever attitude I decide to have impacts my feelings a great deal."

"And this is why **it's important to control our thoughts**. This is the perfect time to apply what we discussed earlier," affirms Paul.

"You're right! My first reaction would have been to try to solve this problem quickly and rush to a solution. But, I think at the moment, it's important to stop, relax, and leave the problem for a while," I add, as I remove my backpack. "Let's have a rest and a bite to eat. We may be hiking for a long time and rushing will only make us more miserable. Look at the forest around us! It's so beautiful and peaceful! When I look at our situation in a peaceful, relaxed manner, there is really no problem in the present. We have food, water, it's sunny, and we are safe. I realize that **my fears are all coming from my mind.** Up to today, I've never thought of controlling my mind. Now I see that my mind has a huge impact on my life". It turns out to be fun! It's dark when we reach the town of Kaysersberg! We're exhausted from several extra hours of hiking, but happy to arrive and to have been able to control our thoughts!

- **Control the quality of your thoughts.**
- **In time of stress, it's important to stop, rest, and be in the present.**
- **In the present moment, there is no stress. Stress is in the future or the past.**

PRACTICE

- Keep identifying and challenging your negative thoughts. You need to repeat the process on an ongoing basis for a long time to change your habits.
- Change your negative thoughts to positive thoughts!
- When feeling stressed, stop, take deep breaths, slow down and focus on the present moment.

Run from anything that gives you the evil thoughts … but stay close to anything that makes you want to do right.
2 Timothy 2:22

To different minds, the same world is a hell, and a heaven.
Ralph Waldo Emerson

Yesterday ended last night. Everyday is a new beginning. Learn the skill of forgetting. And move on.
Norman Vincent Peale

When you wholeheartedly adopt a "with all your heart" attitude and go out with the positive principle, you can do incredible things.
Norman Vincent Peale

To everyone is given the key to heaven; the same key opens the gates of hell.
Ancient proverb

Be transformed by the renewing of your mind.
Romans 12:2

MORE POSITIVE THINKING

Faith is the bird that sings when the dawn is still dark.
Rabindranath Tagore

15

It feels good to walk around the streets of Kaysersberg with no backpack. This morning, we decided to visit the town before heading out. Kaysersberg is one of the prettiest villages in Alsace, with its medieval houses dominated by the ruins of an old fortress.

Our trip is almost complete! It seems natural to walk. I don't feel like going back to my other life. I feel good now. Relaxed, and peaceful. Will I be able to keep this peace in my life?

Ah, my mind is going into negative territory again! Will I ever be able to control it? There I go again, more negative thoughts!

My focus is not right. I'm focusing on the lack, on what I don't have, on what I fear. Again, I realize the value of training my mind.

We stop for coffee and watch the townspeople go by, as I share my recent experience with Paul.

"This morning, I kept thinking that I'll be returning to my previous life, and all that we've talked about will be forgotten. I realized it was my mind telling me this, that I won't be able to make changes in my life and I'll be unable to control my life and my thinking."

"It sounds as if you don't believe in yourself," says Paul. "Do you believe that life and your mind will steal your will and you'll have no control?"

"Yes, that's what I believe. And I have to admit it's not very positive."

"**What you believe will happen!**" Paul continues. "If you don't believe in yourself, you will not be successful. Let me give you an example of what I've experienced. Have you ever run against the wind during a long run or a race? You can react in two very different ways. The usual way (and my usual way as well) is to complain. I say to myself, this is so hard! I'm so tired! I can't stand it! Everybody will pass me! I won't be able to continue. I don't need to say more; you know this style of thinking, and its result."

"Yes, I know the results of that type of thinking. Fatigue becomes worse, I slow down, feel more tired, and might even quit."

"But, Michael, you could also see the situation in a different way. You could say, great, this wind is good! It will cool me off. It will make me strong! I'm good at running against the wind! I feel so good running against the wind! If you consciously change your thoughts in a positive way, even if you don't feel like it, your fatigue will disappear, your speed will improve, and you'll have a pleasant time. Thinking negatively affects our life in the same way and it slowly damages our mind. The only way around this is by doing the opposite and constantly reversing the process by retraining the mind to think positively."

"Paul, that sounds so difficult!"

"It will be if you think that way. You don't have a choice, Michael. If you want to improve your life and have control over it, **you need to seize control of your mind. You are responsible for what you think and what you become!** Negative thoughts and a negative mind only produce negative results. We have to decide what we want in the long term. Taking the easy route in the short term isn't an option."

"I see the wisdom in all of this, but this process seems hard for me to follow. I realize that I think negatively too often and I know I need to change."

Paul reminds me to be patient and keep work-ing at it. "Slowly change your thoughts and ac-cept that it cannot be done in one week. Don't become discouraged. Don't let go."

"Yes, I'll follow your advice. I know it will take time and being impatient or seeking perfec-tion will only increase my negativity. I have an-other question for you, Paul, on a different sub-ject. Since you've left your work, what are your thoughts about retirement? How did you adapt?"

"I don't really like the word retirement. For me, it seems like quitting, withdrawing or the end. I see the present more like a new beginning and a new stage in life. My focus is now different. It's more about giving back and helping others. It's more about personal growth. It's more liberating and spontaneous."

"It's not exactly what I see around me. So many retired people withdraw from the world and re-strict their lives. For me, retirement looks like a scary phase of life."

"Why is it scary?" Paul asks.

"I'm afraid that I'll become like them."

"It's your choice, Michael. You don't have to be that way. You're talking again as if you don't trust yourself. You talk as if you believe you're incapa-ble of managing and directing your own life!"

"Again, negative thinking. I need to change that. It's everywhere in me. What can I do?"

"As I said before, Michael, change takes time, and the first step is to become aware of those negative thoughts, just as you're doing right now. Then you'll be able to change them! As long as you want to change, as long as you believe you can do it, and as long as you keep at it, you'll be successful. It takes time. You need to constantly remind yourself to do it."

"My way of thinking is so negative and insidious. I don't always recognize it as being negative. I need you to point it out to me."

"Michael, you need to learn to do that. **It's a lifelong process to retrain the mind.**"

"How can I develop ways to keep me on track? Do you have any tips, Paul?"

"I only have a partial answer to that question from my own personal experience. I'm not sure if it will be useful to you, but you may use it as a starting point and then develop your own way."

"So what do I need to do?" I can't hide my impatience.

"One of the tools is to put **reminders** everywhere; reminders to have a positive mind or quotes on positive thinking. I place them in my agenda, my phone, and my car. I read them on a regular basis. Another way is to dedicate **one day a week to positive thinking.** During that day, I make a special effort to be aware of my thoughts all day long. I identify them and consciously change my negative thoughts into positive ones. I read books on positive thinking and try to focus my day on positive thinking. I don't even read the newspaper that day; it's too negative. I also take time to record my negative thoughts, challenge them, and rewrite positive statements instead. Writing adds power to the process."

"Are you successful?"

"As much as I want to be or believe I can be! I have to tell you a story that illustrates how the mind works. I recently returned to rock-climbing. My daughter is passionate about it, so I couldn't pass up the opportunity to try it again."

"Rock climbing! I'm not sure I'd like to do that."

"I wasn't sure either," Paul explains." My first climb wasn't great and I didn't go far! However, during the climb, I clearly became aware of how my mind was working. My mind was constantly telling me things like this: it's too high, it's too hard for you, you'll fall and get hurt, it's impossible to do. My mind was very negative, closed to the experience and doing everything to make my experience fail. As I watched the others climb, I had time to "talk" with my mind. My second climb was incredibly better and faster with no fear. I was amazed by the clarity of the dialogue I had with my mind. I was surprised to see how closed-minded and afraid my mind was. But I was also amazed at how easy it was to win over the mind and take control of it. I didn't want to be afraid, sitting down watching others rock climbing. I wanted to be part of it, I wanted to enjoy this new experience, and I wanted to be successful. This is what I said to my mind, and it worked!"

"I need to remember this. My mind is naturally fearful, inflexible, closed to new experiences. Do I want to be like that? No way! I need to challenge all that. Slowly, I'll develop into a different person."

- **Control the quality of your thoughts.**
- **If you don't control your mind, your mind will control you.**

PRACTICE

- **Become aware of your thoughts**. Identify your dysfunctional thoughts.

  Are they positive or negative?

  What is the origin of your thoughts?

  Are they due to a belief inside yourself that is not true?

  Write down the belief behind the thought and challenge it. Is there another way to see the situation?

  Is it due to self-talk in your mind that's not helpful?

  Write a different, positive and constructive self-talk.

- **Choose a day dedicated to positive thinking**. During that day, train your mind to overlook the negative. Identify the good things that are happening to you that day.

  Turn off the TV, Internet, and radio, and don't read newspapers.

  Associate with positive people.

  End your day by making a list of all the positives in your life: today, yesterday, and this year.

Faith is to believe what you do not see; the reward of this faith is to see what you believe.
St. Augustine

Take the first step in faith. You don't have to see the whole staircase, just take the first step.
Martin Luther King Jr.

Very little is needed to make a happy life; it is all within yourself, in your way of thinking.
Marcus Aurelius

Life consists in what a man is thinking of all day.
Ralph Waldo Emerson.

We can't solve problems by using the same kind of thinking we used when we created them.
Albert Einstein

Hold faithfulness and sincerity as first principles.
Confucius

NEAR THE END

Take your life in your own hands and what happens? A terrible thing: no one to blame.
Erica Jong

16

It is time to leave beautiful Kaysersberg. This is the last day of the hike, and I can't help but feel sadness and regret over finishing this trip.

"This has truly been one of my best trips," I say. "Not only in terms of visiting the area, but also for the mental and physical growth I have experienced. It feels like so much has happened during this trip. It's definitely something I want to do again. **Hiking is the perfect activity**! It's good for the body and the mind. I like the peace that it brings me and I've learned how to slow down and enjoy the present. You must feel like that all the time, Paul, now that you have all this free time."

"Yes, it feels great! But, it wasn't like that at the beginning of my retirement. I was surprised to feel some discomfort. Free time was new to me and, in a way, it was simpler when I was busy."

"What do you mean?" I ask.

"When I was working, I didn't have to plan my days, as they were all set." Paul explains. "Now, I have to plan my days, my weeks, and this isn't always that easy to do. Sometimes, in the past, I may have been tired, irritable, or anxious. But after a few minutes of work, it was all gone: the fast and busy pace of the day seemed to erase it all. Feelings are now more real and I'm unable to escape them. They stay with me and it's not always comfortable to feel them, after escaping them for so long."

"But isn't that what we talked about, being in touch with our feelings?"

"Yes, but it didn't feel right at the beginning. And I realized that feelings are there, they exist and are part of my life, part of myself and they give me a message of who I am and what I think in the present."

I begin to reflect on all the feelings I've repressed over the years. I wonder what kinds of messages I've missed, as Paul continues.

"In addition to being more aware of my feelings, I also realized that I had a lot of wrong expectations regarding my new situation. I thought I should be happy all the time now that I could do what I always wanted to do. A bad day and having feelings of dissatisfaction were unacceptable to me."

"You believed that by changing your lifestyle, you'd be happy all the time?" I ask.

"Sort of. However, I realized that a change to my life situation didn't mean everything had to be perfect all the time. I needed to change my attitude and my thoughts."

I'm surprised to hear Paul talking that way. I always believed that everything was going well for him and that he was not the victim of the same problems I had.

"I became aware of guilt feelings," Paul adds. "I also felt guilty about not working as hard as others! Sometimes I compare myself to others and I feel that it's not right to work less than they do. That I am being selfish."

"Why do you think you're selfish? You've worked hard for almost 30 years. Isn't it time to change and do something else with your life? You're not exactly sitting around and doing nothing. You're still helping others."

"You're right, Michael! I need to challenge all of these beliefs as long as they exist. And comparing myself to others actually brings a lot of dissatisfaction to my life. When I compare myself to others, I usually try to take something in my life I don't like and compare that with the appearance of what I like in others. And it's just an appearance. Reality isn't always as good as it appears."

The view of the next village stops our conversation. This is where we will end our hike, but this is also where we'll celebrate the fall season and harvest time. Tomorrow we will have the chance and privilege of participating in the vendanges or grape picking. We'll be in the middle of Alsace's vineyards, in this pleasant valley, doing something that has changed little over time - where human work is still valued and meaningful.

Don't compare yourself to others. It may bring you misery.

PRACTICE

- Identify the times when you compare yourself to others.
- Stop comparing yourself with others, as you don't know their reality and see only appearances.

Each one should test his own actions. Then he can take pride in himself without comparing himself to somebody else, for each one should carry his own load.
Galatians 6:4

All truly great thoughts are conceived by walking.
Friedrich Nietzsche

What a man thinks of himself, that it is which determines or rather indicates his fate.
Henry David Thoreau

Men harm others by their deeds, themselves by their thoughts.
Augustus William Hare

By the grace of God, I am what I am.
1 Cor 15:10

FLEXIBILITY

Therefore the stiff and unbending is the disciple of death.
The gentle and yielding is the disciple of life.
Lao Tzu

17

"What do you mean you don't have a room tonight?"

"Well, sir, we're full and we don't have a record of you making a reservation to stay here tonight."

"That's incredible." Paul is furious. "I called two months ago and made reservations for two rooms for tonight!"

"I'm sorry, sir, I don't have any record of this and we don't have any rooms for tonight. I can phone and try to find you a room somewhere else in town."

"I don't want to go anywhere else. This is where I made reservations and this is where I want to stay!"

"But sir, I don't have any rooms for tonight. The hotel is full."

"That's your problem; I made reservations here and this is where I will stay!"

I feel obligated to intervene. "Now, Paul, let's stop and look at the situation."

"Don't get involved. I made reservations for this hotel. There is nothing more to discuss."

"But, Paul, you heard the front desk clerk and there are no rooms here!"

"That isn't my problem! I have a reservation and I want to stay here!"

After some discussion, Paul finally calms down and we settle into a different hotel further down the street, but not too far away. Paul is silent and I feel the need to challenge him.

"Everything worked out alright in the end, Paul. But this event raises some questions in my mind." I said. "You've taught me all these beautiful principles and you practise them all. I wonder why you reacted in such a way. Are all those ideas worth nothing? Are they just wind in the air?"

"Ah, Michael, I like your questions! Always challenging! No, the teaching and practice we discussed are not wind in the air. On the contrary, because of those practices, I'm a better person. At the same time, I'm not perfect and I'll always have work to do to improve myself. This incident has made me aware that there's something inside me that needs attention. In this situation, I could have reacted differently, but the fact is, I did react this way and I have to learn from this."

"Do you think you'll be able to find out the cause of your reaction?" I ask.

"I have some ideas that I'm trying to clarify. I have very high expectations of myself, perhaps too high. You may call it perfectionism. I extend those expectations to others as well. I have difficulty accepting mediocrity and mistakes in others as well as myself. This attitude prevents me from being open and accepting reality. I hate to admit it, but this makes me inflexible, refusing to accept that mistakes and imperfections are part of life."

"I have a similar struggle myself," I say. "I used to be easy going, open to new and spontaneous ideas. But now, I notice some inflexibilility in the way I am. I wonder why? Could it be the effect of aging?"

"I don't like to say it's age-related, as that absolves me of responsibility and, at the same time, it isn't true. My inflexibility relates more to the lack of mind training that we talked about before. If I don't train my mind to be open and accept reality, my mind will become stiff and inflexible. My mind naturally will get out of shape. And like an untrained body, it will become lazy, tired and unable to handle daily life. It has nothing to do with age. Again, it's a question of attitude."

I'm glad to be talking about this, as I've noticed so much inflexibility around me and I add, "I've also noticed that inflexible people stop learning. They stop seeing other points of view, and they restrict their lives. This is the best way to become narrow minded and intolerant."

"You're right Michael, and I totally agree that my reaction wasn't appropriate. The only thing I got out of it was anger. I need to challenge myself. I used to be open-minded, but now I seem to be closing my mind slowly to new experiences. This event really helps me to understand a part of myself that needs attention. But how do I develop flexibility? How do I become more flexible again?" Paul asks.

I have some thoughts to share. "You develop flexibility by doing things you've never done before. You force yourself to do things you would never do. For example, if you go to a restaurant, order something new, something you've never eaten. Try new experiences on a regular basis. At meetings, sit in different places. During discussions, accept others' opinions as other valid points of view. Don't think they are wrong and you are right. Think both of you are right and explore new ideas. Developing flexibility is an endless practise. Another good way to **develop flexibility is by travelling**. Travel to a place you have never been and do things you have never done. This is wonderful for flexibility. **Enjoying a day of flexibility** is also great. During that day, I do all kinds of new things. I try to go through the day in a new way. I get up, and instead of reading the newspaper, I go out for a walk and go out for breakfast. I continue the rest of the day with no specific routine, so everything is new and different. This is a great way to develop flexibility. Going through a day like this feels like a mini holiday and is very refreshing."

- **It is important to be flexible.**
- **If we don't train our mind to be flexible, we will become closed-minded and rigid. We will stop learning, being spontaneous and having fun in life.**

PRACTICE

- **Plan a flexibility day at least once a month.** During that day do all kinds of new activities. Go to a new restaurant, try new food, travel to new places, visit areas you have never been (even in your hometown).
- **Explore other points of view.** Don't be afraid to look outside the box. Accept new ideas and be willing to discuss them with an open mind.

The World is a book, and those who do not travel read only a page.
St. Augustine

Travel and change of place impart new vigor to the mind.
Seneca

Travel is fatal to prejudice, bigotry, and narrow-mindedness, and many of our people need it sorely on these accounts. Broad, wholesome, charitable views of men and things cannot be acquired by vegetating in one little corner of the earth all one's lifetime.
Mark Twain

Be a Columbus to whole new continents and worlds within you, opening new channels, not of trade, but of thought.
Henry David Thoreau

Employ your time in improving yourself by other men's writings so that you shall come easily by what others have labored hard for.
Sophocles.

OTHERS

To do more for the world than the world does for you - that is success.
Henry Ford

18

After the relative solitude of the past several days, we are among people again. We're getting instructions on how to pick grapes from Seppy, the owner of the vineyard. We learn that "rotten" grapes are precious and need to be in a different pail from the regular grapes. The "rotten" part is covered by "noble" mould that is essential to making a high-quality wine.

There are people from everywhere in Europe, who come for a day or more. It's fun and joyful. Everybody is happy. I'm sharing a row with someone from Eastern Europe and across the vine, while cutting grapes, we discuss the difference in lifestyle between his country and France.

I can't stop eating those grapes! I've never tasted such delicious fruit. These are not like the grapes I buy in the store.

The weather is warm and the morning fog melts away, unveiling the village below and vineyards extending forever.

The best part of the day is to come: lunch in the vineyard! It's a celebration of the sun, the heat and the harvest. Most of all, it's a celebration of friendship. We're all talking, laughing, encouraged by the new wine flowing. It feels good to be here.

All of this is foreign to my life.

When did I celebrate at work?

When did I celebrate what I was doing,

what I was achieving?

In the speed of life, I forgot to celebrate what I did well. I forgot to celebrate friendships, and even the joy of working and being alive!

It will be great to bring this new knowledge home with me to celebrate my own "harvest" on a regular basis!

It is with joy that I'll leave this beautiful part of France. It's time to go, but I know that I'll be back soon. I feel like I am leaving a little of myself here, but also taking with me a little of this area - its joie de vivre and art de vivre. The latter is an expression I really like, living well is an art. That is a beautiful way to see life!

Paul drives me to the airport. I'm grateful for the time we have spent together, for the week in the outdoors, and for the sharing and learning.

"This trip was perfect till the end."

"I agree, Michael, thanks to you!"

"Thank you too! It's always great to reconnect, and we need to continue this."

Despite our speed, cars are passing us in a flash, as I add, "Look at the speed we're going! We spent a week with a top speed of five kilometers per hour and now I feel like we're not even moving at 160! Is this an indication of how my life will be tomorrow?" I still have the same concerns I had before.
How will I avoid living at a fast pace?
How will I remember all we have discussed?
How will I cope with everyone rushing around at the speed of light?
I feel like I'm the only one with such concerns!

Paul replies, "You feel alone in this, and it's true that failure is more likely if you are isolated. However, I believe there is a way. For several years, I've belonged to a **small group** of six to ten people who want to change their lives and to have more control. We usually meet twice a month for a few hours, to discuss our life experiences."

"What do you talk about?"

"It depends. There are no rules. Sometimes we choose a subject that we all need to work on, such as positive thinking. We all do some research and at our next meeting, we share our results. Then, we commit to make at least one positive and practical change in our life, based on our discussion."

"And what happens?" I'm interested in this new idea.

"Then we have a follow-up meeting and we challenge each other to fulfill our commitments to change. At other times, we choose a book to study. The possibilities are endless. Being in a group opened my mind to new ideas as well, and it helped me to keep my commitments."

"This is good. This is very good! And I know a few friends who may consider starting such a group. I may need your help, Paul, to set this up."

"Keep it simple, is the best advice I can give you, and be persistent. Experience will help you, and it doesn't have to be complicated. Be sure to call me anytime and I'll be happy to help you! On the other hand, if you don't want to belong to a group, why not find a **Life Coach** in your area?"

"A Life Coach? What's that?"

"A Life Coach is someone who helps you move to the next level of excellence in your life. You meet in person or on the phone to gain direction. They will hold you accountable for achieving your goals. It's an ongoing process; it may last several months. I've found coaching to be very effective."

"I will certainly investigate that as well."

At the airport, people are running in all directions, with no apparent goals. This endless movement infiltrates everything under a background of incessant noise, and I wonder if I belong here. It feels so foreign to me.

As I fly home, Paul's messages are still in my mind. I need to remember what I've learned during this trip. I need to keep practising, and develop good habits. Too often the law of least effort is my way. Doing what I enjoy first, what is quick, what is easy or what is familiar. Too often, I'm a prisoner of my own bad habits, my material possessions and even my own thoughts.

I need to be more conscious of what I do. This is not an option! I don't have a choice. If I don't incorporate this into my life, my mind will become rigid, negative and closed to new experiences.

Doing this by myself seems so difficult, while the idea of starting a small group seems very good. I not only need to apply what I have learned, but I need to go beyond my own person, my own self-interest! It's time to increase my openness to the world and others. There's so much to do!

And this is my next challenge: to go beyond myself, give to others and share some of the multiple gifts I have received in my life. I feel that this is my next life stage; something new that I need to discover. And to be able to see the needs around me, I need to slow down.

I realize that speed has been the enemy in my life. Speed that is so addictive and exhilarating is also speed that can kill, not only kill on the highways, but also in my life. It destroys my awareness of the present, and makes me unaware of the needs around me, in my relationships, in my work and in my life.

As I return to my previous life, I bring with me some new questions:

> What is life all about?
> Who am I serving? Myself or Others?
> Who are my gods? Cars, money, houses, fame, myself?
> Who is my God?
> Beyond helping others, this is also where my mind, spirit, and heart need to turn.
> And as I fly home, I realize that in the middle of the flowers and the birds,
>> God was with me!
>> And I was with God!

TO BE CONTINUED

It took many years to get here,
and will take a lifetime to finish.

Do something for somebody every day for which you don't get paid.
Albert Schweitzer

Our deeds determine us, as much as we determine our deeds.
George Eliot

There is more happiness in giving than receiving
Acts 20:35

We need to find God, and he cannot be found in noise and restlessness. God is the friend of silence. See how nature, trees, flowers, grass - grow in silence, see the stars, the moon and the sun, how they move in silence ... we need silence to be able to touch souls.
Mother Theresa

Ask and it will be given to you, seek and you will find; knock and the door will be opened to you. For everyone who asks receives; he who seeks finds and to one who knocks, the door will be open.
Matthew 7:7

You are only young once. How long that once lasts is the question.
Anonymous

It is not because things are difficult that we do not dare; it is because we do not dare that they are difficult.
Seneca

I don't want the cheese; I just want to get out of the trap.
Spanish proverb

Philippe Erhard

One more quote (mine this time!):

There are two types of travel:
Travel on the earth-it is best done on foot,
Travel inside oneself- also best done on foot.
Travelling inside oneself is the most difficult trip, but also the most rewarding, and most interesting.

APPENDICES

Appendix A: POSITIVE FEELINGS

In chapter 10, we talked about identifying feelings. Positive feelings are sometimes more difficult to experience. For this reason, I have compiled a list of common positive feelings.

It's good to read them from time to time to develop awareness of them and when we focus on them, they will expand.

Affectionate	Hospitable
Alive	Hopeful
Amused	Humorous
Appreciated	Joyful
Accepted	Kind
Brave	Lovable
Calm	Loved
Capable	Loving
Caring	Loyal
Cheerful	Passionate
Cherished	Positive
Comfortable	Peaceful
Competent	Playful
Confident	Pleased
Content	Proud
Courageous	Quiet
Curious	Relaxed
Delighted	Respected
Desirable	Safe
Eager	Satisfied
Enthusiastic	Secure
Excited	Serene
Forgiving	Spontaneous
Free	Supportive
Friendly	Sympathetic
Fulfilled	Tender
Gentle	Trusting
Generous	Truthful
Glad	Tolerant
Grateful	Willing
Great	
Happy	
Honest	

Appendix B: RECOMMENDED READING

This is only a partial list. At some point it is important to stop reading, and start doing, and applying what we have read. These books have had the most influence on me:

- **The Bible**
- **Man's Search For Meaning** by Viktor E. Frankl
- **Feeling Good** by Dr. David Burns. The focus of this book is depression. However there are very good sections even for non-depressed persons. The section on distorted or dysfunctional thinking is especially useful and worth reading.
- **Anxiety and Phobia Workbook** by Edmund J. Bourne. As indicated, its main focus is anxiety, and therefore useful to all of us. It is a great book, very complete and practical.
- **The How of Happiness** by Sonja Lyubomirsky. A very practical book, full of suggestions for improving one's life and backed up by scientific studies.
- **Turning The Mind Into An Ally** by Sakyong Mipham. A beautiful book on the mind and how it functions (the galloping horse description of the mind comes from there) and it is a great book on meditation.
- **The Power Of Positive Thinking** by Norman Vincent Peale. It is one of the first books I read about positive thinking. It was written in the 1950s and is still very useful with good advice and many practical applications.

To contact the author:

www.erhard.ca or phil.erhard@gmail.com

For information on coaching:

www.erhardassociates.com